The Memory of Birds
in Times of Revolution

*These fragmented thoughts and images
are dedicated to the memory of
my dear friend, Rob van Gennep,
by way of continuing
the dialogue.*

Contents

Good dog.
reportedly Lenin's last words

Life is probably easier if you're a dog.
Peanuts

The Memory of Birds
in Times of Revolution

Writing the Darkening Mirror

'I have drunk, and seen the spider.'
Shakespeare

1

Out at dawn with a mighty yell. Shout of joy? Scream of acute distress?

Life a trip. The traveller — arriving at the station, cut off at the intersection — not the same one who was so keen to disappear into the landscape. 'From one two will always come', said Mao. And one is digested by time due so that, if you will pass me the expression, the excreted leftover or marker may be but poorly related to the substance which so vigorously entered life's verbal grave. 'Of the two orifices through which the dejection of being human passes the mouth is the worse' — an Arab proverb.

As the ground of received wisdom gives way under your feet you become more painfully aware of inconsistencies in that made-up individual discerned in the mirror, the presentable one that you tried to memorize and project as the historical first person singular.

We have been deceived by the big pictures held up by prophets and charlatans — communism, fascism, nationalism, liberalism, democracy: this conspiracy of ideologies ostensibly imposing a pattern upon history. The big kill intended to confer a purpose upon small death.

Our dreams rotted at the seams, even though we sometimes still swing an arm and a leg as if clothed and capped with dignity. For the time being, smoothed down by our destiny as consumers of the surfeit, we are obliged to compose with a socio-political environment shaped to the 'rights' (I mean appetites) of the rich and the greedy strong. Global integration deploys its cape to flash the lining besmirched by private estrangement. The relations between the haves and the had have been brutalized — be it within the walls of individual nation states or over the hedges of protected wealth when dealing with the Other, the inhabitants of those exotically miserable continents constituting the ghostly subconsciousness of history.

There are few stays against barbarism. It has become the moral slip of the tongue to allow as easily for the implosion of a distant country of savages as to kill for a thimbleful of crack. What handholds left? Could we, should we even, expect directions on our journey through the bowels of existence? Is there anywhere to hide? We aren't even permitted the mercy of being lost. The unexposed moons of our minds were screwed by Freud and Co. fishing for amputated joy, and now we distrust the very correctness of our most intimate emotions.

It is the privilege of the writer to bring awareness to the obvious. But the self that only comes to awareness and therefore into being through expression is finally strangled by the umbilical cord of creation. The more you write yourself the less you know. Writing comes in the place of experience, stitching an opaque surface through and in which less and less can be seen. The process obliterates the purpose. The burning ship goes under in the mirror's depths. You are left with a sense of relief, with your shroud as token of survival, with the book chucked like a wreath to bob on the waves. You are left with the task of polishing the stone so as to burnish the image of burning in the mirror.

We are split personalities — sequentially, often simultaneously. We may turn our back in disgust on previous selves, but they hang around our neck like lovesick shadows. Like Rwandese attempting to walk away from disappearance. Like Cuban *balseros* paddling towards Babylon's shore of neon-lit illusions.

What I call 'self' can only be the thread stitching change to change. And death is no ending, it is the final self. The end product when light at last falls short.

In other words, what one brings forth from the self — which is change incarnated — is death. The other words exhaled constitute the breath of death. 'Life' is anyway only the illumination of the infinite variations, nuances, explorations, backtracking, and slownesses of dying.

Writing is a messy way of committing suicide, cowardly involving as many people as you can reach. It is the trick of smashing the mirror in order to other the self. A Chinese saying notes, however, that it is not definitely bad luck to lose your horse. Eat the horse and bury the mirror! To hell with paradise!

2

Maybe life is one long flashback. (I'd be inclined to call it a *blackflash*.) Allen Ginsberg suggests we live the memory of a long-ago dream. As we move over the edge of our century into a new millennium and look back, it must be with dismay at the blood-smeared road we travelled.

To name but a few salient characteristics: We have been blessed by two world wars, the development and the use of mass annihilation weapons, totalitarianism with deportation and generalized torture as means of government, barbarism, Mickey Mouse culture, revolutions and civil wars and colonialist wars and wars by procuration and peace-keeping wars, fast food, disempowerment by bureaucrats controlling regulations and technocracy, the corruption of political processes and the distension of public ethics, the destruction of utopia and the decay of idealism, the diabolically refined paroxysms of racial hatred and bestiality, television as the pornographic purveyor of insatiable desires, the contamination of our natural and social environments, Swiss banks, the enshrining of reasons of state with the accompanying secretion of security oligarchies. The French Minister of the Interior (and Police) argues that democracy stops where the reasons of state commence . . . Look at the indicators of martyrdom, or markers of obscenity: Franco, Afghanistan, Stalin, Hiroshima, Baghdad, Shoa, Andreotti, Apartheid, Hitler, Somalia, Sarajevo, Stasi, Vietnam, Guernica, Chernobyl, Cuba, Khomeini, Palestine, Liberia, Lebanon . . .

Our intelligence is but a make-do defence to mask the despair of the human condition. Can we really face and decipher ourselves? How do we come to terms with the knowledge that most of these crimes against humanity were perpetrated in surroundings of advanced culture? Were the Germany of the thirties and, later on, Britain and France and Portugal and the United States not steeped in fine music and beautiful works of art and literature of the highest order and good philosophy? So then, were the horrors of genocide and wars against the weak committed despite the cultural environment — or, with arrogant superiority, as necessary prolongations thereof?

One could certainly evoke alternative traditions by naming Gandhi and Mandela and Guevara, Brecht and Charlie Chaplin and Frida

Kahlo and Malcolm X and the Zapatistas of Chiapas. One could mention moments of humanism and resistance and velvet revolutions. Perhaps there's even democracy with a human face somewhere. But this is not much of a consolation as we flounder in our own shit.

Racism, although no longer official state dogma, is rampant practice, reinforced by the xenophobia of Fortress Europe witnessing the shattering of its illusions against barriers of the possible. With the shame of poverty once again looming – 22 of the 35 million people out of work in the over-developed North are in Europe – dark urges are seeping through the cracks in the façade of liberal civilization. The break-up of the Soviet empire is still convulsing old hegemonies like Yugoslavia with ethnic dismemberment. Disarray, political cynicism, diplomatic pusillanimity, impoverishment and religious fanaticism are waxing. There's a recrudescence of ancient plagues like malaria and tuberculosis, and the rapid spreading of new scourges like AIDS. Art is giving way to the postures of Culture and the wrapping of Reichstags. The art of living is arbitrated in consumer troughs called supermarkets. Reflection is replaced by the globalized inanities of a CNN cancelling out values and destroying the capacity for memory and discernment and citizen participation. And Africa, like a sinking vessel of heathen slaves, has slipped over the horizon of political awareness, to be left to the obscure mercies of the IMF and the World Bank and death merchants dumping their obsolete military hardware and their nuclear wastes.

We are the world. But we are not of the same world, nor are we all equal. The relationship between North and South (or the West and the Rest) is that of crude difference between the strong and the weak. Whatever is to the advantage of the powerful becomes a necessity, and then a criterion, and then the only way to conceive of solutions, and then a truism, and ultimately a moral value. The exponents of a free market system, meaning freedom for the strong, are occupying the moral high ground. Public intervention is depicted as unfair to free enterprise, and corrupt because predicated upon political manipulation.

The circle has been squared: 'democracy' equals capitalism. *Realpolitik* begat *Realmoral.* We forget that capitalism can only survive if it expands – there must therefore be profit and loss, discrepancies to create desires, fewer winners and many losers. There's no way, seen from the North, in which the suffering of a black can weigh the same as that of a white. The double standards are underlined in South Africa where the world media are now waiting for the vicarious thrill of an expected slaughtering of the whites – which will only be fair retribution, according to liberal European moralists washing their dainty hands of any responsibility. And in the Middle East even a hundred Palestinian lives do not equal one Jewish settler.

How can we pretend to be of the same world when, for example, in a context of global expenditure having multiplied sevenfold since 1950, 468 dollars per American is spent on advertising in the USA compared to fifty cents per person in China? (Except that the Chinese should consider themselves privileged to be thus spared the filth of greed.) When developing countries can only barely manage their foreign debts, let alone foster long-term growth? When the number of official refugees rose from 2.8 million in 1976 to 18 million in 1992, and the estimated number of people forced from their homes but not from their countries now stands at 25 million? When some 94 per cent of adults in the rich world are considered literate as opposed to 65 per cent in the poorer parts, and less than 40 per cent of African women can read and write? When, in 1991, the total gross national product for the 500 million people in Sub-Saharan Africa (excluding South Africa) was 205 billion dollars, about the same as for Belgium's 10 million people? When on average nine out of every 1,000 children under five years of age die in the United Kingdom, whereas they will be 292 per 1,000 in Mozambique and 253 per 1,000 in Sierra Leone?

Little surprise then that the South does not share, in equal measure, the North's concern for ecology, population increase, energy consumption, public health, human rights and war.

It is not my purpose to exonerate the South from blame for these inequalities. True, it has been dispossessed, history never existed and time seems to turn back upon itself, the people there are apparently free from the obnoxious ideal of limitless progress, and life has been whittled down to the noble art of survival. But the South is not just some continent of the subconscious populated by exploited but noble Natives, on which idle Europeans can project their dreams of mystery and of magic. It is only too easy for Northern manipulative influences to amplify the existent corruption of the leaders, the élite's feeding frenzy, the alienation of the intellectuals, the propensity for looting and killing.

5

Only the poor can break the cycle of exploitation and dependence. Power makes stupid. Neither religion nor ideology nor even art will permit the dominators to understand the underdogs. Utopian collectivism, just like free trade capitalism, is a European export notion nurtured on Northern greed and uncertainty and dogmatic dreams. The Rest must hold their own, not because the West will be so kind as to allow justice in international economic dealings, and dignity to those living on the periphery of their concerns, but because they will have no choice. It is only by generating and mobilizing Africa's capacity to think from its own reality, to transform its conditions so as to live within its means, that the grip of European charity and paternalism and cultural cannibalism (and the *pleasure* Westerners get from feeling guilty), so corrosive to Africa's self-image, can be loosened.

For this Africa will have to rethink the very patterns of its social organization. Are nation states really the best model for encompassing tribal realities? How come 80 per cent of the population – the peasants, the women – are totally absent from the political processes which concern them? Africa will have to invent its civil society as a field of balancing political powers.

Using cultural awareness in the North as in the South, we shall have to find new ways of undermining old and new hegemonies of control, of deconstructing the nouns and the norms of power, of revalorizing the discredited concepts of internationalism and solidarity.

Perhaps, too, we can then enter an age of doubt – with more uncertainty, probably even with unrest, but also with more humility and less hubris. And thus come to understand that interdependence and fraternity are necessary survival attitudes.

3

The last lap of the journey to the end of the line is going to be a tight squeeze. Why go on? When you look closely the ego is a black hole. A very attractive nothingness. Perhaps I'm just falling into the classical trap of reading my creaking joints as heralding the end of the world. (In truth, my death will naturally mean the end of time. How could it be different? When the clock stops there is no more passage. When I said this to my old accomplice, Ka'afir, he snorted and described it as African reasoning: 'For Africa has time but no history.')

And when the self is other, why continue? Because of some unslaked curiosity to see what will come next. Because — surely — of attachment to a few people, a few places, a few hours. To stick, for a while still, with this *savoir-vivre*, the simple joys of smelling the sea, of drinking in the shade, of touching lips. The temptation is always there to enter the waiting *nada*. It will not be a defeat. But she can wait a little longer.

South Africa, it is now often averred, is the 'feel-good story' of our century. Indeed, a kind of inverted miracle did happen: the transition (in these pages I tried in my own fashion to trace the territory and the trajectory and the traditions and betrayals of transition) was less bloody than feared. Mostly, I think, because of the majority's capacity for suffering, their patience, their confidence and trust, by and large because of their willingness to forgive.

I remember what a moving experience it was to be in the country earlier this year during elections. The infirm and the aged with subterranean thoughts and dead eyeglasses, bent low over trembling walking-sticks, peasants and proletarians dressed in spotless poverty, rich madams in furs from the so-called mink and manure suburbs — all waited patiently in line. Some had been waiting all their lives. At last we were given the opportunity to be bonded, even if only temporarily so, as one population of the same country tied by the carrying out of a shared civil privilege. It was a supreme act of remembering and reaffirming dignity — although the messy memory of responsibility for past atrocities was weirdly absent. A new present tense was being born in a welter of killing. I wanted to be sure that no power, old or new, could ever again deprive the millions of people of their individual shares in the future. But did we really put down the past thus crossed out? And what unsatisfiable needs will the future unveil?

In any event, I was glad to be finally shot of the load of being a 'South African writer', moreover an exiled one. I take it as axiomatic that most people were not, are not, interested in about 70 per cent of what my painting and writing could be about. The long years of apprenticeship taught me (I hope) to keep a free mind uncluttered by interest or position, refusing to be used. (And often lazy.)

I have come to know that such freedom can be a dangerous reincarnation of unfreedom, since it drives you as an arrogant and ignorant giver of lessons into the margins of society. (But it is so *good* to undermine the centre . . .) I do know now that my painting and writing could not have made much difference to the struggle: you can neither sublimate nor console others in the rawness of their lives. Artistic creations do not reflect life, they are *life-like* – and constitute a life of their own. I'd love to think that I participated in the making of dreams. The tracing of the true movements of the heart, though, is the drawing of a broken and twisted line of existence. This in itself embodies a function, like the bird warbling. We all share a need to see our fall marked.

Was it art for art's sake then? No, I still believe it was (and will continue to be) for the sake and from the bowels of humanity, from the darkness of our being and by the light of our passage on this glittering planet. Art as an existential desire to recognize ourselves through the metaphysics of the real and the invention of the known. Art, at most, as the transmission of certain images and metaphors which stay and strain our deeper dreams. Art as a discipline of being. Like breathing. Conveying neither good nor bad. Art as a most basic measure of solidarity. Seeing is a prerequisite for action – even if it doesn't mean that we will ever be strong enough to oppose the fabrication and the selling of arms and motorcars.

What remains is the feel of being and the sense of process, this desperate attempt to deconstruct decomposition. Along the way ghost images of the selves and the Other may emerge by way of exploring the slips and the cracks, the facets and the faultlines in the face of the real. The texts which follow will present more or less chronologically the finger moving over that face. Writing is to think fire and then to poke in the ashes for absence.

As a *nadaist* and a *nomad* I have been luckier than most writers. If you agree with me that it is advantageous to realize as cleanly as can be that there is no single immutable illusion of self to cling to, and that the only revolutionary question is the Other, then I certainly had more breaks than most. In fact, I've been served a king's swill of that food which helps stimulate the search for positioning when you want to sharpen the recognition of the outlines of *nada*! There are so many stories and pictures that need to be shaped! I had to roll away this stone, this 'autobiography of spent ideas', from the tomb – to get to the freedom of poetry.

Power corrupts. Weakness destroys even the dividing line between corruption and moral probity. It will be good if we can learn non-power. Which is no weakness. It will be good, for instance, if South Africa could withstand the temptation of being the death merchant to a continent. The exciting challenge (and the miserable fate) we face is the obligation to keep on inventing ourselves – in terms of identity and authenticity and of usefulness, in deciding upon the weight ascribed to historical memory, in keeping alive the creative tension between sharedness and differences: if only to find a sustainable balance. Already there has been exhilarating movement – from exclusion to tolerance to accommodation to inclusion (which may be where we're getting to now) – but to survive, this process must proceed to transformation.

To remain critical. To test the boundaries of ethical consciousness. Never to be on the side of the angels. To give face to the Real by writing the darkening mirror. To be ready to be wrong. To listen to the grass growing. To work from the periphery while having in mind the ghost of a moral centre. To remember that seeing is a way of turning over the sods even if you risk finding rotten fish in the soil.

A girl fighter from Zimbabwe, called Freedom Nyamubaya, in a poem reflected upon the rigours of returning to a liberated land:

> Never again will I rest
> Always on the go to nowhere . . .
> A dog at dinner,
> A combatant the rest of my life . . .
> But struggles go on
> Still on the road
> An endless journey

Capri, November 1994

Tortoise Steps

Somewhere during my time inside I came across the remnant of a verse written by the Buddhist philosopher Maitreya. He lived during the fourth century. The lines, translated this way and that, are probably partly eaten by time and frequent transcription:

> It is not suggested
> That all the elements are unreal,
> Nor that they are all reality;
> Because there is being
> And also non-being
> And (again) being:
> This is the Middle Way!

The lines should be read against the context of arcane arguments, then in vogue, regarding the nature of reality. Is it not still the quest of our flow of awareness — this need to apprehend, explore, define and extrapolate the concept and the realness of reality? Is it not that which keeps propelling us forward?

What strikes me about the innovation of the Middle Way, the way I understand it at least, is that it embodies the necessity of movement; it is a line along which you *go*. Not a *fuite en avant* circumventing and obscuring irreconcilable contradictions, running away ahead so as to run out of road, as it were — but, rather, a suspension of the extremes, admitting that all is possible and so is nothing, and then recognizing the practical reality that you have to move along, that it would be futile to sink into the static stance of waiting for the opposites to be resolved, that only the new shoot escapes the duality of the bean's two lobes, that clarity of mind is a peristaltic practice and not contemplation — the way the finger writing the moon is not a satellite of the earth and the word 'moon' on paper can never shine since paper is not light-fracturing infinity but born of trees. That life can finally only be lived. Let me add before leaving the track — and for this you have to look at Laotse and not at Maitreya — that it is also said: If you can lose it you never had it, and, Unless you can laugh at it, it is not the Way.

I started with the old Indian by my side for several reasons. One: the theme proposed – *The Writer and Frontiers* – evokes the need for definitions. We are always on the way to definition, or *in* its way, for it is hard not to stumble over the words, as the blind Borges may have called out while exploring, and thus creating, the labyrinth. Nothing, neither I nor you nor the lines linking and separating us, will ever be drawn to the full. Not even beyond death. Especially not beyond death. The word, as with Sisyphus, will ever and again fall away into the void. It is better to keep an open mind, or an unclosed grave. (Pardon me the tautology.)

Two: he who says 'way' is implying 'geography'. Permit me to introduce the proposition of a Writer's Land. In so doing I shall show no reticence in being obscure, no shyness in calling upon notions not shared by you even if they've been worn away to a shine, no hesitation in plotting areas unknown to you or pointing out ethical outhouses shunned by you. Who says 'geography' as a writer must be talking about a moral territory outlined by a frontier of responsibility. Therefore of a territorial imperative. And immediately one evokes the old reflex thought of 'the enemy'. Why not? It is customary, and an inexhaustible source of deep security, to have enemies.

It is anyway too late now to conform to post-modernist norms and to prostrate myself before television muck. Writing, when applied judiciously, can also be a form of self-flagellation, with the advantage at least of chasing you away from the tables where hormone-fattened calves, poor-white water-swollen chickens, fall-out powdered spinach and other camouflaged antibiotics are guzzled down. These goodies being mostly too expensive for the writer's purse. You may wish to point out that it is far more taxing to eat good down-to-earth vegetables, fish without mercury, milk without strontium, Granny Smiths that smile at you with the wrinkles, unradiated radishes, olive oil that's not meant for tractors, tomatoes that are not cloned in Dutch greenhouses, butter which is not from the Common Market Surplus Mountain. You really want to be different? Pay! Pay! Pay!

I shall open brackets here to say – since we are touching upon the twin notions of *responsibility* and *choice* – how very startling it is to read the statements of multi-national spokesmen, those grey-voiced parrots, telling us not to worry about radioactive grain being transported across Europe, about poison produced in Basel for agricultural use, about the nefarious effects for babies of Nestlé's powdered milk: those products are meant for export to the Third World only! (If only we could give them the Rhine as well . . .)

Three: to return to my road – it is allowed, recommended even, to go back and do the same stretch all over just to see how different it is each time, and to stretch the retching – to look at *where* the line runs between us, *what* it consists of, *what* it defines or excludes. Borders are as many scars, in places still sensitive to the touch, likely to erupt unexpectedly, over which one is never too keen to linger.

Last: to underline again the importance of the only white stick the writer can use to poke at the surroundings: write on! walk on! If you read in this the attitude of the activist, a plea for sublimating the seemingly unresolvable extremes of day and winter, a call to move along and create the facts (reality can only be apprehended through the imagination) well beyond the confines of Writer's Land too (but who is to say where the line of writing stops?); if you read in this a proposal that the writer should be a 'mule', a *passeur*, a *contrebandier*, a smuggler, a raider prodding other people's scabs with his pen: please do not hesitate. You will be right.

There are self-evident meanings pertaining to our subject that I do not wish to dwell upon. The obvious one needs mentioning only. I don't know whether any borders were ever welcoming, pleasant latitudes of a *dépaysement* to be crossed, the markers to an expanded experience of, at the very least, *Verfremmdung*. Now they seem to have become restrictions, the perimeters cf some xenophobic paranoia, walls erected to repulse the outcasts and keep away the hungry. What has become of the ideal of cultural refuge? We had been told of European generosity flowering from ineradicable democratic instincts. Then we look at the way the Swiss moo during their recent referendum concerning the status of foreigners on their money-rotted soil; we hear French politicians suggesting with sly lips that to become French at eighteen when you were lucky enough to have been born in the national and metropolitan and Republican territory, from foreign worker-ant parents, and provided you haven't smudged your record with minor peccadilloes the way some of your native-born French peers might have, and on condition that you speak French *comme il faut* – then to opt for nationality will mean recognizing that to be *French* is an *honneur* which must be *mérité*.

You Europeans have structured the world according to your appetites and fears and you have scant appreciation of what it may mean for a foreigner to make his often illegal way to your shores after many sacrifices and slain crocodiles — from a remote village in Mali, say, a venerable land if ever there was one, where humanism still matters (except that the universal context is now white: be realistic, it is said, let the free market forces separate the weak from the strong) — with the forlorn hope of being able from here to help his starving clan survive. Does Europe ever admit to the honour of receiving such people?

Send us your money, you tell them; let our jaded senses enjoy your rhythms of perversion and your toned-down dishes; make your labour available at competitive prices; pull up your yams and sow soy for our cattle so that we can make you eat our butter; straighten out your debts by culling your people, the IMF orders; prove to us that you don't have AIDS, you say — but in God's name *don't* come Allah-iAkbar us, *don't* rape our ears and our women, *don't* come slaughter your sheep in our bathtubs, stay *away* from us! Look up to us and be free! Or would you rather have the gulag system beckoning down liberation road?

This, you must understand, I only mention in passing since it is not the purpose of my discourse. Neither do I wish to belabour the example of the frontiersman coming to mind unbeckoned — the exile, the émigré soul-stutterer, the language jumper: the Nabokovs, Becketts, Baldwins, Brechts, Miloszes, Ciorans, Brodskys, Kunderas, Patricia Highsmiths, Durrells, Greenes and other Millers. (Whatever happened to Solzhenitsyn?)

To be concerned about frontiers nowadays, to flog a dead horse, is to be investigating clogged horizons in an assembly of deadened souls where the debate of ideas has become the phantom practice of bloated belches. Nevertheless, it remains my hobby-horse in a world where there is the telescoping of ancient miseries and injustices (famine, racism, neo-colonialism — to name but a few), and the progress of 'new poverty', structural unemployment, 'modern' forms of barbarity such as television, pollution, arms selling, the *Gross-Europa* idea (being the sanding over of local variations or discrepancies or differences or quirks or histories, with the rhetoric and the unstoppable logic of multi-nationalist monopolism, the flattening of horizons). Plus, of course, the universal total nuclear suicide pact. Stone the thought!

Let me tease out a few threads and warp the woof somewhat. When I hear 'the writer and frontiers' I understand 'the writer and responsibilities'. To wit, the recognition of his limitations, the casting net of his concerns, the extent of his investigations, the barriers he transforms into barricades to pathetically attempt stemming the flood of media-conveyed and -purveyed stupidity.

Central to this examination is the identification of the writer and his society. More precisely – the function of the writer within his environment. To me it is clearly a question of interaction, of the one being defined in relationship to the other. Within this framework we can look at the history of cultures, the development of ideologies, the countdown of struggles. (Do I need to remind you that Marx, Freud, Fanon, Cabral, Nietzsche, Jung, Gramsci, Trotsky, Darwin, Plato, the great Arab historians, Paul the Tentmaker . . . were writers first and foremost?)

Writing, paradoxically, is not solitary creation. Of course it is finally the sound made by one hand clapping, but always the expression of a *lived* experience (even when in appearance the life of the mind only), of attitudes and positions and the absence of these, shared inevitably with at least part of the community. One may say that every writer lays his own egg but it is never a unique act. The hen is the consciousness, the conscience, the history (thus the experience); the egg is the product, the creation, the writing (thus the consciousness). And who is to say which came first?

My minimum definition of the writer would be: he or she who creates written things transformed into as many realities as there are readers. Writing then is also the making of mirrors, the forging of hopes, the depository and deposition of memory, the insistence upon guidelines, iconoclassicism, the making of prototypes from stereotypes, a grave game fraught with consequences, the small talk of sorrow, inventing sunsets, the sacred gluttony for the mother tongue, a way to redistribute differences, a flight of fancy. True, it is at the same time a glaciation of guilt, and often the dream gets chucked out with the dirty water of art, and writing can be a plagiarism of thinking or a silence made of bangs and snorts, and no poetry has ever allowed a paralytic to walk (except with the crutch of the mind). But the white fire exists. Poetry is like leaving a pebble outside your front door to mark your residence and when you return in the evening you find a stone. And isn't the moon a stone?

I repeat – and now I'm precisely talking about frontiers: the writer works with the essential and incompressible protomatter: awareness. He is a consciousness-expanding agent.

The writing, the writer, that which fashions the beak through which he sings, those who share the song ... As for me, not only am I of the South African variety, but I'm an *Afrikaner* Azanian pariah to boot, thus tissued from a people who *par excellence* got themselves entangled in a frenzy of frontier tracing, creating weals, cutting into the living fibre of family and nation.

And immediately I face a suppurating history where all problems exist in their most acute form; where everything and its absolute opposite are true; where definitions are perforce part-time and shifting; where the bloodlines of language and experience meet and engage — ideally in the process of *métissage* and metamorphosis from which not only new cultural identities and a creole beauty such as Afrikaans may emerge, but also more sensitive moral criteria. Alas, the clashing of horns is also a confrontation producing the seemingly endless brutalization of human intercourse, a ceaseless spilling of blood and burning corpses. There, writing could be the line contouring if not synthesizing the known and the unknown, a frontier between decency or tolerance, and barbarity. The barbarians were always with us. They (to plagiarize Pogo) *is* us.

In South Africa we have, as in Lebanon, the *institutionalization of horror.* In sociological parlance the South African system is total, that is, a self-enclosed deviation of the norm, a country-wide prison or madhouse; medically speaking a community exhibiting the syndrome of a metastatic cancer in a body whose immune system has become deficient, *inter alia* because of the token resistance by way of anguished existentialist bleating or other decadent adaptations of the intellectuals. South Africans and Azanians alike are killing themselves in the name of survival. You cannot have an omelette without breaking the eggs: this is an old South African saw; we invented the original wisdom. In fact, breaking is the name of the game, be it egg or head or heart or memory. Resistance to crude exploitation has furthermore been sapped by *de facto* foreign condonation. I can say it in a million ways but it always comes down to this: Apartheid (to call it by its folkloristic name) exists *also* because it profits international capitalism, *also* because it corresponds to a deep-seated universal white racism. Any shopkeeper worth his salt will tell you today's takings are more important than tomorrow's risks and to hell with the inheritors.

15

Now, on the other hand, the moral ostracism applied by some to that country is, excuse me, obscene — designed to exculpate the distant begetters of the monster. I have come to the stage where I don't *want* you to talk about Apartheid unless you also recognize how it flows from our shared history, how it dovetails with elements of your ideologies and sentiments, and how *talking* about it can mentally and morally neutralize the unimaginable horror of it. I refuse to continue being a party to the condemnation of Apartheid, which leads only to moral posturing. We are fattening the monster on our outcries of shame!

Why is it so difficult to admit to parentage? An old Afrikaans song created, as most of our Afrikaans culture, by the 'Coloureds' (we have 'Cape Coloureds' the way you find 'Peking duck' or 'Delft blue' under other climes) says: 'You argued in vain / You argued in vain / As long as that child lies in the shawl / He will look just like you!'

Do you know there are areas in South Africa — I'm thinking for example of Botshabelo — where the unemployment rate reaches 70 per cent among surplus people dumped there because they don't fit into any known Bantustan (even our border-madness knows its limits and can go haywire); and that the Taiwanese, Hong Kong, South African and Israeli firms implanted there pay their workers the equivalent of forty French francs a week while getting from the central government a weekly subsidy of seventy francs per qualified worker? Do you see why it is difficult for me to keep on writing towards sanity, to exhibit like this our bloodstained ropes for your delectation?

Never confound the Middle Way with equanimity.

It is a matter of legitimacy. There is to my mind no way in which the international community can acquiesce to the political or moral legitimacy of the present South African régime — not unless we accept that the relations between nations can by nature be monstrous, and that we must think away this vision of evil in the name of state interests.

Where does the responsibility frontier of the writer run under the circumstances? If I deny them their legitimacy — because I have to do so if I don't want to puke all over my fine intentions and besmirch my beautifully crafted pages — even though the frog cannot fart at the moon, should I therefore support or close a disillusioned eye to 'legitimate violent resistance'? Can I go with the deaths when faced by an enemy who refuses to allow any other alphabet but that of killing to exist? If not, what then? Is it legitimate that the writer confront this question the same way other citizens do? Or must he be singled out? Should he not be involved in the mouthing (or the mealy-mouthing) of ethics then? But surely he must since he speaks by and of and to people.

The responsibility of the writer is not so much one of literal *meaning* but of social and moral implications. Do we still remember how obnubilated we were by the incendiary tracts of a Mailer or a Marcuse? We justified our stance or our cowardly dance in the light of such writings. They wrote and we lit the fires. Some of us waved Mao's little red thoughts about our heads as excuses for not thinking. But if not this way, how then?

Is thought being? Must thought take the place of being? Must we overthrow and plead for non-rationality, seeing how the virtuous tides of rationality washed us up on a beach of bitterness? But with what forms of control then? Am I – to exploit a medieval dichotomy – advocating the 'heart' against the 'light' of reason? No, I'd rather suggest the personalized practice of non-duality.

Like everybody else we loll, fat gluttons in front of our blue flickering magic-boxes, idly fingerfucking the controls to flick from channel to channel and zapping the magic of our imagination. We are vaguely irked by the withdrawal from reality symptoms. We think we are being exposed to a greater array of *choices*. But there is this weird dialectic (as a friend of mine, talking about the mass-mind-marketing of literature, pointed out recently in a Dutch magazine): that as the possibilities increase so the alternatives are narrowed down. More! More! More! Therefore: Less! Less! Less! We now avoid polemics and suffer the cultural voracity – alternately stuffing ourselves and then sticking a finger down the page to regurgitate the junk. Are we not subjected to ethic consumerism?

The writer is not protected from banality. On the contrary – and this is a typical frontier problem where he runs wild with the words thinking he's extending influence over concepts; I know what I'm talking about – rare are the occasions where he succeeds in avoiding the traps of cliché and bombast. Coming from the writer the deception is the greater. One would have thought him or her fleeter of foot than to be thus quicksanded by the obvious and the stale. And yet, we must insist upon the choice, the *right* to not know, to not have an opinion, to be wrong often, to keep a shut mouth at times, to talk through our necks with easy minds, to be mediocre. Not to know the answers and to admit it is to be privileged! We writers are spoilt children!

Ropes, lines, definitions, frontiers ... Already I have played out my line too far not to be returning with a crow's nest.

We are going through a mutation of time experience. The more we know the less we remember. The clearer the lessons of history become the more avidly we rush towards annihilation. There is speed-up. Instant obsolescence. The writer is admonished that he should master the new techniques, shape up to the form. What is new? The banalization of information through television, the large-scale moulding (or rather moulting) of attitudes via the media in the service of state political control and big-business interests – by means of their henchmen, the makers of opinion and the hawkers of bland products. No intensity of texture, and a strategy of structure aimed at mindlessness. The medium – being multiple, an omnipresent intruder, forced to capture attention rapidly and superficially because of the competition – the mediatic form formularizes. Suddenly we are discovering millions of empty hours that need to be filled with emptiness. We are force-fed on trivia and images so mushed by the media – there can be neither relief nor context outside that of sameness – that they course through us with the aftertaste of artificial water and the glow of greyness. We become inert. Our attention span shrinks. We become querulous ...

The writer on the other, slower hand still may indulge in more ancient and more intimate modes of communication. The shape he tries to unveil demands of the reader some participation, some attention, the transformation or the appropriation of the matter. I'd say it is an old expression of responsibility, and a pity that it should be lost – not because it is traditional, but because the loss will be that of a faculty of remembering, of possible excellence. The writer as keeper of lost time.

Then the writer as explorer of the limits of writing. Meaning: reconnoitring the frontiers, sniffing along all the barriers, lifting a proprietary leg, shifting the parameters, extending the spaces of liberty and getting to sense the spacing thereof. Meaning: to keep on identifying our reference points, our restrictions, the borderlines of our influence, our conscience of the effects we may be having. I cannot subscribe to the demand for orthodoxy but neither should I as the writer be permitted to get away with the consequences of my wordthoughts, which are as many actions. No self-censorship but self-criticism, humility, a healthy dose of ridiculousness, ignorance in small measure, mediocrity even. (That comes without effort.) Meaning: that there's no reason for the writer to be allowed a *carte blanche*; a white page should suffice. Authority, the City, let's say the hydra-headed Order, should insist upon contestation, should demand it of the writer, to help prevent thought and its expressions — thus the form — from becoming iced over.

The real revolutionary question is: What about the Other? To hold onto one of the essential frontiers, the navel-string running between you and me, this quotation from Leopoldo Maria Panero in *El Pais* of 25 April 1987: 'Here then already the perception of the other is a question of life and death ... We must avoid the pitfall of: one unique reality where the other is nothing more than a symptom of nothingness (*la nada*). Thus, when a man is cured, he pretends to have forgotten. Freud, on the contrary, wrote "Wo es war, soll ich werden" — there where it was, I shall become ... Which means to say that I'm neither mad nor cured but rather a man who, like Jonas, comes naked and frightened from the chemical whale, carried as a memory to all the people I know.'

It is of course not enough to rail against the descending darkness of barbarity and media alienation. One can refuse to play the game. A holding action can be fought. Alternatives must be kept alive. While learning the slow art of revolutionary patience. We have to explore the subterranean tracks, the hidden rivers surfacing as eyes elsewhere. The writer must acquire frontier-consciousness.

Can Ocells, May 1987

Nelson Mandela Is Free!

Nelson Mandela is free! The word rustles like a breeze through the townships, whispered in awe, shouted in triumph from mouth to mouth, from shack to box-house. Did you hear? People wipe their eyes in wonder, greyheads laugh, babies squawk, dust rises from under the feet of young comrades running the streets with the black, gold and green banner. In the *veld* small boys with bobbing loincloths whistle shrilly and hurl twirling sticks at recalcitrant beasts. By noon they will take the shade under a thorntree to tell tall tales, each in turn a proud Mandela.

In Qunu of the green hills the clan will be sprucing up the graves of Nosekeni and Henry Gadla Mandela. This is where 'Buti' must come to sleep the night and cleanse his hands before the slaughtering of the sacrificial ox. Napilisi, his nephew, says: 'All I know is he was put in prison because he wanted equal salary for all.' In his wayside store, Makgatho is trying to capture his father's image on the television screen the way one attempts to net a butterfly.

Nelson Mandela has been released! Old women lift their skirts to step up to the memory of a youth of rhythm and stomp. The reeds bend with the light. Old men marvel at the trembling of history and drown in thick beer this day, and the hump of accumulated days scarred with the pain of poverty. On Robben Island, in Pollsmoor and Victor Verster and Zonderwater and Brandvlei and Barberton and Diepkloof and all the other hell-holes of humiliation, prisoners bang their tin plates and chant: 'Man-de-la! Man-de-la!' And in the quieter quarters of dehumanization the politicals stand taller to look the warders straight in the eye. Old guards remember and talk softly to their old wives. Torturers put a finger under a sweaty collar; they are thinking about changing their addresses. Security experts pore over the store of tapes and secret photos with which they hope to blackmail the leader: Mandela with Coetsee, Mandela with Viljoen, Mandela with De Klerk, Mandela laughing with his head thrown back, Mandela relieving himself, Mandela in tears.

Poets are biting their pens. Yuppies, caught in a traffic jam, wind down their windows with a bronzed hand to shout: 'Mandela!' Cabinet ministers take medicine, and look at one another in distrust. It is hot on the beaches; sun-reddened farmers from the interior squat attentively around portable radios. On the mountain slope above Cape Town harbour 'bergies' wipe their stained mouths; one bum reminisces with the toothless grin of timelessness: 'I remember the day King George came to town . . .' Burly men in khaki garb snarl insults at their mocking labourers. Behind closed shutters a hit-man thoughtfully oils his rifle. Maybe the earth is heaving, the sea swollen with expectations. Old dreams pour forth.

We have liberated Mandela! Grown fighters sob. Professionals plot new allegiances. Ancient companions review their splattered lives. 'Now the problems start.' His wife is working out which dress to wear for what occasion. Go-betweens are offering two minutes, four minutes, three smiles and a nod, dollops of his availability . . . for a price. In Havana, Moscow, Lusaka, London – wherever silence caught up with the exiles, some people will remember to visit the places where the bones of tired strugglers are mouldering in foreign soil, to whisper: 'Yes, it's nearly finished now. Soon we shall be going home.'

All over the world children wriggle out of their mothers' wombs, screaming at the light, to be named Nelson Rolihlahla Madiba Mandela. In African capitals students wave hand-printed placards defying rot and corruption, and perhaps imperialism too. Miners straighten their backs and wipe their brows. In glittering salons of the OAU, bureaucrats try to get a grip on events as they sip at small cups of coffee and feed the prayer beads in a trickle through their fingers. There are holes in the carpets. Musicians weave the magic mantra of Mandela into their melodies in Wolof and Swahili. Pygmies along their forest tracks, Bedouins in their encampments wrapped up against the winds of the sun, hunters along the flanks of simmering volcanoes – all invent the past and the limitless future stretching all the way to freedom of a man who once lived and who was called Mandela.

Nelson Mandela is free! The news reverberates around the globe. Jesse Jackson and Margaret Thatcher and Helmut Kohl and George Bush screech and scratch to get a morsel of glory. In Warsaw and Berlin and Accra and London the lost and scattered children of South Africa, and some from Azania, the broken warriors expelled from the movements, are getting drunk and obnoxious. In India a

fat wrestler changes his name to that of Mandela so as to draw
larger crowds to the fairgrounds. In New York a trembling hand
writes: 'Dear Mister Mendalla, my husband is lamed, we don't need
much, I have no-one else to turn to . . .'

The powerful of the world issue bloated statements, and confiden-
tially ask their ambassadors: 'How long will he last?' On Caribbean
islands, in a swirl of rum spat out and cigar smoke, he is incorporated
into the Voodoo Pantheon to unite forces with Legba and Victor
Hugo and Toussaint L'Ouverture and Baron Samedi. Mummified
dreams are being dusted down. In Japan a new doll comes on the
market with the features of the world's oldest prisoner. In Peru the
Shining Path guerillas cheer and shake their bitter machetes. In
Central Europe, intellectuals ask: 'Mandela who?' Somewhere in
Cambodia a political commissar gives Mandela to the Khmer Rouge
as example and justification. In Western cities young revolutionaries
with feverish eyes and death at the throat, shout: 'Mandela!' hoping
that this revolution at least will not be aborted in blood.

Old gulag inmates taste the salt on the wind, and sigh, and are
bothered by something in the eyes. In poorhouses, in hiding places,
in dungeons, in old-age homes, people murmur: 'So it hasn't been
for nothing after all.' An impresario is putting together talent for a
sing-along. In Korea and Finland they spell his name wrong. On
French television, marathon talkers miraculously find a second breath.
People swell up with self-satisfied indignation as they use Mandela
as a battering-ram to get at the adversaries.

Literary agents are sending urgent faxes. Lovers suddenly break
down and start sobbing in the hollow of their beloved's shoulders.
The night has become small. A Hollywood mogul is hollering
instructions down the line to offer him any effing price he wants, as
long as it is for ex-clu-si-vi-ty! Multinational bosses reassess strategies and instruct their minions to have advertisements of welcome
published immediately. A child writes a birthday card and mails it to
Nelsin Mondale, South Africa. Obsequious secretaries silently enter
offices to place files on leather-topped tables. Smirking presidential
advisors twirl non-existent moustaches.

An old man emerges from prison. He went in an activist, he
comes out a myth. He worries about his prostate gland, his notes.
A horizon lights up, he brings hope, and he never knew the world,
nor the soft caress of empty days under drifting clouds. If he ever
did, he no longer remembers. Perhaps there is now a little more

sense to our dark passage on earth. He has kept his body and soul together with pride and the impossibility of love. He will succeed. He will fail. He lives. He will die. Nelson Mandela is opening a door.

Paris, February 1990

Fragments from a Growing Awareness
of Unfinished Truths

(for Tsitsi Mashanini)

'I have no consolation, and I reek of contradictions.'
A. Artaud

Ladies and gentlemen, members of the police, the security police, National Intelligence, Military Intelligence, Civil Cooperation Bureau, Special Operations, Municipal security, spies, agents, infiltrators, grasses, grey shirts and grey shits, moles, operators, hitmen, handlers, car bomb artists, paymasters, Broederbonders and other intriguers and plotters and schemers and wanglers limited, inner-sanctum strategists, public saints and private sinners, deeply troubled intellectuals, Total Responders, ex-torturers, inquisitors, confidential advisors, stable-lads, courtiers and courtesans, frustrated functionaries and jacks-in-office, future élite of the people, fellow-travellers, deserters, runaways, movements groupies, hangers-on, henchmen, musketbearers, quitters, hands-uppers, scabs and scallywags, blue-eyed boys, moral rearmers of the National Party, federated Afrikaner culture carriers and cultured crust and cultural workers and vultures, blethering bell-goats, lapel nibblers, anus suckers, traitors, backstabbers, masters of gossip and character assassination, agitators, troublemakers, floor-cloths, scenario constructors, yuppies and buppies and immaculate yoof generation, rugby players, dog-catchers, helminths, bar-room heavies, hemeralopic hermaphrodites, haemorrhoid heroes and smelly snails, reporters, negotiators, patriots, undertakers, resurrectionists, sacristans, beadles, clerks and cowboys and choralists, contact cultivators, informers, closet revolutionaries, wankers and voyeurs and aesthetes and gourmets, leaks, facilitators, unidentified sources, co-opted and structured flunkeys, canaries and converted consensus-seekers, professors and doctors and eggheads and go-betweens and bathroom toughs and teat-tutors, stupidity stirrers and Stellenbosch students and star athletes and midnight streakers and hysterical halleluya-singers and highway whores, high cockalorums and gibberish gobblers and coccyx cognoscenti and coitus cohorts and capped wheateaters, witch doctors and lay preachers and divinity students and alligators, seedsocks of the nation, hedonists and heathens and anarchists and kitchen communists and Bolshies and fish hawkers and green fanatics and faint fighters and objectors and heavy hearts and hail-fellows-well-met and bum steers, buddies and mates and chums and chinas and ministers and other poophole pilots, companions and comrades and ex-convicts, brothers and sisters – in short (because I don't wish to be ill-behaved toward anybody), my dearly beloved fellow South Africans:

I stand before you in threefold mortification. This country has always affected me in ways that I find difficult to come to terms with. Now I have to realize that its ways have become too heavy and too *other* for me to assimilate, perhaps because with time the assimilator lost the flexibility of growth. I go for a run on the mountain and the old smells of vegetation from long ago, although unidentified, the swishing bluegum trees and the first plum blossoms, this rush of familiarity brings a peace and ease that I can feel only here – and at the same time the experience is tinged with strangeness, even estrangement. A French philosopher said the punishment for a man who loved women is to love them still. I am in love with this country as if it were my first infatuation.

Deep down everything I know belongs to me – was the sense of being myself not forged here? – but now it is a deceased sense, a kind of apocryphal subconsciousness which shrivels my dreams and gives an absent-minded resonance to whatever my hand finds to do. I always saw myself as radical: a life of fits and starts, fuckups and breaks; sometimes I charged with fixed conviction from the trench, often I turned tail and fled. I must simply accept that I'm a poltroon and get out of the way. This chiaroscuro, the pine-cones and the crepuscular odours of mountain flanks mixed with that of the sea, the ancient recognition of people's gestures and the smiles in their eyes – it all hurts too much. That which for so long was a known intimacy is now a close confusion. Like this the dead must feel when he rises again accidentally. It is no longer my country.

The first embarrassment: to flaunt my private hesitations in a foreign environment. My anchors, even the sea anchor, have ripped loose – how can I then pretend to take you in tow? I now understand why I was so reluctant to come, because for me it means taking leave of revolution, of a love relationship, of expectations; it implies a farewell to public involvement. Before it becomes too sombre and lachrymose I must add that the revolution will self-evidently continue on her route – she doesn't depend on me, after all – and I do not in the least intend to retract from earlier positions, nor do I wish to rub ash in my beard and bewail the good old days. The cruellest characteristics of the good old days are still with us. The murders have not abated; the indifference and the arrogance of the rulers are still in place. The poor are poorer and the rich richer. The scars and the moral contamination of their illegitimate state are evident for all here to see. The looting continues. The struggle too, and the deviations and corruption unleashed in the process are becoming starker by the day. I'm not suggesting that you shouldn't do as I did, but I do affirm that there's a time to come and a time to go, and my own small moment of truth – which may seem like withdrawal – has arrived, even if only to proceed to a deeper acceleration.

Perhaps the surrendering of my estate is not all that private. It could be symptomatic of the muddled transitional phase you find yourselves in. Then my second source of distress would be that I am so confused, that I have already repeatedly spoken too much, and now I have little sense to impart or contribute towards a clarification. This would be excellent: the time of the oracles and prophets and gurus and judges is finished, and I should hope that of the commissars likewise. You need to be bewildered, again and again, until such time as you're obliged to think for yourselves. If you have to be stupid, at least be so with your own authentic foolishness. Rather this than the disgrace of being manoeuvred to cover up somebody else's clever follies. Why should you ape them, or gambol after any leader to holler *vivas* for Africa? Those pulling the strings will in any event see you as a herd of dunces and dolts.

South Africa's dominant culture is one of co-optation. There are still too many zones of silence, of accessary muteness, of reciprocal moral blackmailing living on hereditary guilt and the need to be humiliated. We don't take each other on, we don't even feel each other up, we prefer to handle and to manipulate one another.

I'm looking for revolutionaries, not believers. In reality the revolutionary ethos of loyalty and honesty, and the decent purging of differences while respecting diversity — not to morally squeeze the outside world for hand-outs — does not yet thrive in South Africa.

Nothing to say and nobody to hear that nothing. Only experience brings comprehension and we cannot learn — neither from history nor from guidance or parrot talks. Even the myth — the mantra mumbling or the artefiction — of the viability of a communist state in South Africa will have to be realized first and then dismantled from our own experience, since the implosion of East Europe evidently has no impact on local minds.

My third quandary: that I push myself into a ridiculous and marginal role with this vacuous prattling. Worse, where I'm now shaking the circus sawdust from my feet, I shall be obliged to show signs of an encompassing wisdom preferably milked from Culture's udder, that secular cow, and of this I'm perfectly incapable. I now know less than in the beginning except for a few refrains, the after-sounds of the cuffs around my ears. Ideology is the mirage of a dream shimmering beyond the horizon. There is neither release nor solution, the dream is dead. Utopia was plundered and then torched, like an empty bottle store — yet change is inevitable, transformation hobbles along, the projection of alternatives (including dreams) remains functionally compelling; we are part of the process confronting the steep learning curves from Marxism to a material reality.

My mother always said it's not befitting for a blind person to throw stones in the bush — just now a dog will jump out! Over and again my mouth falls open at the pleasures of Afrikaans, at how it can talk a dog from the undergrowth. If I were to say: 'I'm stepping *on* the dog', then I'd better high-step sharply in order not to be bitten; if, however, 'I step *in* the dog', I'm a goner, the trap would have sunk its snarl in my shoe, and the stench will bring a blubbering of curses to my throat.

I hope I didn't come here with the missionary's narcissism. I don't intend lending a hand in the unseemly wrestling for Stellenbosch's soul, even less to point the Afrikaners in a given direction. That would be futile and vain. I'm here quite simply once again to plait my voice in the chorus of a national debate, the plaintive croaking of frogs . . . We remain unfinished — part private, part public — and for self-knowledge we must defer to how others see us.

The themes which keep emerging are time, movement, relationship, identity, change, narrowing vistas, peripheral vision, crusts of

experience, timorousness and ruggedness and rough patches, responsibility (for what? to whom?), expectations – shared and existential –
clarity, communicability and the how and wherefore of it, the
constraint of perception, the prescriptive view others have of you,
lost opportunities, wrong options, the dead weight of eschatology,
the teaching of last things when your saddle-sore soul knows there
are only beginnings and never conclusions, the concrete but also the
limited and the relative . . . The more I try to think 'the public thing'
the more an obscure observation point is secreted, that chaotic
combination called 'I'. Everything and its precise opposite are
equally true, as also the imprecise opposite (one should not dis-
criminate). I have problems with definitions, but in order to get a
grip on phenomena as they rise on the skyline of experience, in
times of exchangeable readings from the lap of a consumer civilization, with the writer as smuggler of perceptions – or, since we
are born of the partisan equivalence of language, to be calibrated
by conventions – definitions are indeed needed! More tentative
than this I can hardly be without covering myself in dust and
silence. Nor more private. (Looking elsewhere for definitions I
already found that ethics constitute the private parts of aesthetics.)
So, in the linguistically related search for a digestable description
one is once again obliged to brood over 'the Afrikaner' – and in
Stellenbosch of all places, where suppression, oppression and repression received their degrees of excellence, this cultivated and learned
and respectable and relaxed and jovial and self-satisfied and ultimately ostentatious and foppish environment where the matter was
ostensibly settled!

The little I know I wish to transmit. And kick off by stepping in
the dog when I say I have no interest in the superstructure of a
search for power – that *lambada* indulged in by Government and
ANC – but, rather, in the infrastructures of meshing, the mechanisms
of reconciliation and a growth toward an ethically concerned South
African identity, from the bottom up. The aim, as far as I can see,
remains to transform the State into a democratically legitimized
framework for all citizens. To get there we'll have to clean out the
stables of our history by taking responsibility for the dung, and to
do this we shall have to break down the blind walls protecting
(enclosing?) Afrikanerhood, or, rather, Afrikaner culture. The party-
state is a repressive and alienating structure – I think by definition,
for it is far from being only locally true. En route to the destruction

of the State — which, to my mind, is what National Reconciliation ought to be about — there are a number of non-negotiables (known in South African politspeak as 'bottom lines'): a redistribution of wealth but a reordering of the possession of production means as well; opening to all equal rights and the same opportunities of empowerment — politically, economically, socially. The historical processes which call forth socialist thinking remain valid, and the need to think socialism is as urgent as ever. Participation in the process can advance, I believe, through the prioritization (ugh!) of a left alternative schooled in vigorous independent thinking to counter hegemonistic tendencies. Not that you need to be sectarian; on the contrary, to mesh implies collaboration on unitary programmes and projects, on condition that such collaboration be supported by binding democratic agreements. But it is imperative that you don't go look for consolation in the arms of a new establishment, now that you're finally withdrawing limply from the existing one. You can't just switch horses in midstream because there's blood in the water.

To put on unadorned sandals and Mother Hubbard maternity frocks and 'native' African shirts, and then to go on bended knee to tongue-swab the comrades' superior backsides, all the while pretending you're eating humble Damascus pie, is really only white paternalism with another pale countenance. Just as a Stalinist by any other name will always remain a manipulator — because it is assumed from the outset that the goal justifies the means, that the Party is the avant-god élite knowing best what is good for 'the people' and therefore must lead, that any reality can be confined by its correct interpretation, that democratic centralism is user-friendly to free thinking and individual responsibility, that utopianism is a science — just so the white Calvinist, even when clothed in 'revolutionary' garb, continues to wallow in predestination, in the necessity for atonement and for abjecting and subjugating the inner self to the cause and its leaders.

I'm reminded of the story of great-uncle Andries Afrikaner, who decided, when already leaning well forward in trembling years, to throw himself upon a second marriage. The tender mare's name was Vryheid ('Freedom'). Great-uncle Andries Afrikaner had seven boys from his first union, and now, when it was time for the nuptial night, for the breaking in of Vryheid, you might say, he summoned his offspring and told them: 'André, you and Philippus and Ampie must come and help your pa up tonight. And Jan, you and Braampie and Bottlehead and Hamteef will tomorrow morning help Pa down.'

'But why must there be three of us to lift Pa in the saddle and four to take Pa off?' André (the cheeky one) wanted to know.

'Because I'm going to resist', the old man growled.

Let me put myself in your position. Why must I believe that my contribution to nation building or national liberation should be adversely defined by the fact of being an Afrikaner? Is it a condition or even a given which the Xhosa or the Sotho must overcome? Admittedly, we Boere transport a hell of a lot of corpses in the boot. It implies that, to reach the desired destination, we shall probably need bigger cars and drive somewhat more carefully — but this is a difference of degree, not of kind.

Afrikaners must be deprogrammed and given the option of moving away from *Die Burger**, South African state television, the syllabuses of Afrikaans universities. There's an evil conjunction of opinion-spinning spiders (journalists, teachers, commando officers, pastors) whose water and lights of authority ought to be cut off to prevent them taking hostage yet another generation of Afrikaans-speaking South Africans in the cynical end-game played out by the Broederbond and National Intelligence. As the returnees one by one come into contact with this land's harsh realities — the humble truth of existential decay, of an absence of political education and structuring as opposed to the grassroots myth of mobilization, out of ignorance or worse, the fraud perpetrated (on both sides) in pretending to the outside world that the country is ripe for burning and revolution — so the white natives must again and again be brought to a cognizance of backyard South Africa, that is, greater South Africa's basic realities. Not only to take notice, but to partake and participate. I know it is asking a lot of you to shift the focus from black servants in the kitchen to black comrade commanders in the parlour. Nonetheless it cannot be reiterated often enough: the only pathway to reality runs through participation, at every conceivable level, in the processes of clarification and remodelling. Nobody asks of you to stand in line for entry tickets to the never-never paradise of camaraderie, but to knowingly become sinew and nerve of a creative project in the community at large where people will take

* A conservative Cape newspaper published in Afrikaans.

reciprocal responsibility for what they've done to one another, and are still doing.

You — we — are the inheritors of reality, and reality is an expanding field of awareness, and growth implies growing up and growing together, and conscious growth is expressed in involvement. In the friction and symbiosis between you and the Other a new dynamic will be released for which you will share accountability. Many of you have been doing so since a long time, there are those here who know all about aching sorrow and hardship and bitterness and killing. This subterranean Lethe of engagement must become a Nile of fertilization. South Africanness is an itinerary (and a topography) of becoming in the making. It wends its way through the dismembering of apartheid: to have a hand in the memory-making of the greater Othering. By taking apartheid apart we make each other. If we wish to be at home as conscious constructs of transformation — and not just the empty cockles of pre-destination or historical. determination — we have to tame the art of making melodies of our differences. We should learn how to bequeath power, and remember about the forces of illusion instigating new patterns of behaviour. South Africanness is to take part in the quest for the embodiment of an imperative metamorphosis towards justice. You must move away from subservience to the authoritarian 'Broeders' (as in Broederbond, or Big Brother), to the egalitarian embrace of fellow-'brothers'; from kitsch culture and cults and myths to critical creativeness (which may well include kitsch and myths and cults).

In the beginning we had the madness of conceptual Apartheid (segregation, sundering, isolation, the undoing of synthesis — curious the satisfaction that can be obtained from inflicting punishment on others, and maiming the self!), then followed the dark years of dirty history when the last remnants of decency were scrapped to erect a wall of Total Response against the Total Onslaught tides, and when the country was left in the filthy hands of military megalomaniacs, paranoid policemen, prick politicians and professional hit-men. The froth of that unholy broth is still boiling over.

I have no quarrel with the ox-wagon sentiments of Treurnicht and Terreblanche.* What does it matter if they want to move

---

* Andries Treurnicht, leader of the Conservative Party, now deceased; Eugene Terreblanche, the clown commanding the far-right Afrikaner Resistance Movement.

against the stream? Undoubtedly they too, from the fog-shrouded recesses of their past-tense dreams, are contrary participants in shaping the future. What does count is that no one will ever again be able to halt this movement towards broader equity. Of course liberation hurts. I always believed that only the long freedom struggle of black and brown South Africans could precipitate the release of whites from the confines of their fears as self-repressing masters. And I'm convinced that there is enough constructiveness in the Africanness of the Afrikaners to enable them to contribute positively to a bigger South African dispensation. The Afrikaner is not a threatened species. Perhaps because the sands have run through the white man's hourglass of ruling. (What difference will fifty years or even three centuries eventually make to a country's story?) Defeat will save us! Perhaps we have a special contribution to make (from insider knowledge!) in taking to the knacker's yard the monstrous remnants of the rule of oppression.

I can even come to terms with my being an Afrikaner. All these years of dawdling by the fleshpots of Paris − although I was mostly hanging about in the back row − did not make me less Afrikaner, South African and African. On the contrary. One only needs to evoke the names of Leipoldt, Bram Fischer, Betsie du Toit, Beyers Naudé, Allan Boesak, Stephanie Kemp, Uys Krige, Jakes Gerwel, Jan Rabie, Vernon February, Hein Grosskpf and Ampie Coetzee, Adam Small, Marius Schoon, Antjie Krog, Martin Versveld, Johan Degenaar, André du Toit, Van Zyl Slabbert − this list can go on for long − to know that the spectrum was always accommodating enough for you to assume your Afrikanerhood effortlessly.

Now there's talk of a National Compromise, a country-wide reconciliation, like a plague of locusts. It is important, it is the road forward one would opt for, on condition that we clearly understand the grounding of conciliation. If it were to be about two forces cancelling each other out and now reaching a compromise for future collaboration − if, in other words, it is about the ANC and the National Party sharing power − then I'd say: Let's fight on. If, however, it is about gutting the crimes committed (not only by the government), destroying an evil system, fighting old and new totalitarian inclinations, committing ourselves to the moralization of politics, South Africanization and Africanizing − hence to healthy nation building, with reconciliation and democratization concretely promoted in all spheres and at all levels, and if such a national contract could be a launching pad and not just some No Man's Land – then I say: Let's move with the article!

What are we going to do about History's Big Know? When people were hurled out of top-floor windows, stomped or beaten or electro-shocked to death, when bulldozers flattened flimsy shelters, when dogs were set loose upon people, when children were shot at – we *knew* it was murder. When tough guys were ordered abroad – to Vietnam and South America and the Middle East – to be taught the more unsavoury tricks of counter-insurgence, those who sent them *knew* what purposes would be served by such a conditioning. The ministers and their ear-whisperers, the department heads and commissioners and the permanent secretaries and generals and colonels – they all *knew* that they were the tyrants and violators intent upon stripping the state of any moral standing or justification for continued existence. The judges and the magistrates who had before them in the dock those who had been tortured, and who were going to be tortured again, to whom the police lied without flinching – they *knew* what was being done behind the walls. The Members of Parliament with their nifty Protestant moustaches, and the spouses on their arms in full billowing sail for the annual celebration of *arrivist* vulgarity in the Company Gardens – they *knew* whose tune they were singing and the true theme obfuscated by the warbling. The government hacks calling themselves journalists, living like leeches on the National Party's inner thigh – they *knew* of the moral decay, and all they did was to close another eye and open another bottle. Or when they referred obliquely to the rot it was in a code that only ministers of the cloth could decipher. Particularly the clergymen and other pedants, yes, they *knew* well enough, and closed their eyes to cross the road and continue prayerfully on their way. The ambassadors-at-large with the slippery hands like fresh fish, they *knew* and pretended not to.

So many people are educated not to know. Smart alecks there were in ample numbers, but how many will now admit to being and having been in the know? Some assassins in the pay of the Civil Cooperation Bureau apparently didn't know who they were working for – they were killing for the hell of it. University rectors hand in hand with so-called security services intimidating one and all on the campuses to preserve the order which must allow for the indoctrination of the élite sent out to administrate the pagan population, mayors with their very own spies in grey shoes, broadcasters with their special talent for lying and judicious editing, liberal company bosses covering up for the State's agents through fictitious paysheets, pissed roughnecks around barbecue fires, student leaders 'taken into confidence' – all *knew* of the blemish. People were seduced or forced or compromised to take part in the plot. The whole Afrikaner establishment became entangled in a conspiracy of the arbitrary, and there they remain. They were the boys who had to deflect the Red Danger. Not so? Wasn't it for state security? For the survival of the Afrikaner and the continuation of Afrikaans and the protection of civilized standards? Who wanted to know that people had their limbs broken, their eyes gouged and their breaths snuffed because of ignorance and frustration, for the sadistic pleasure thereof, out of a complex of inadequacy and inferiority, seeing that God's face was veiled, to wreak vengeance on a shit life?

Those white warlords, they *knew* there never was a Red Peril. To them their actions were part of a plan to transform the state in a reign of terror. But we actually all know from childhood already how to hide cruel realities under the sheen of decency. Were we not schooled in the art of feint and make-believe, from the pulpit, in classrooms and bars, through Afrikaans newspapers and cultural neoplasms and political *gauleiters*?

And now? Now nobody knows nuffink. We continue living with the same authoritarian structures. The end product can only be something like the barbarism of the security agent responsible for the bomb that blew off Albie Sach's arm in Maputo, which tore his belly and minced his face, when he says: 'We made a nice little sauce of his arm, now didn't we?' Or the cynicism of administrative assassins appearing disguised as poodles before a commission which will mimic judicial inquiry to find them blameless on casuistic grounds ... Maybe we should learn how to screw each other with great sympathy.

As in a Breughel painting we must see to it that everybody in the procession makes it home – the halt must help the lame along, the deaf lead the blind, and give to those who have no walking sticks an AK 47 to lean on. Conciliation is not an ejaculatory prayer or a Sunday commandment; it is a complicated technique, it involves feeling one another for Africa, with unclean hands.

Maybe 'revolution' is a fearsome word. We are only in another difficult phase of the liberation process. There was the Boer War as struggle against British imperialism, this century's initial forty years with a measure of opposition to capitalism, the successive campaigns of national awakening led by the unions and other black and brown and Indian formations. Then came the sixties with the birth and deployment of national liberation movements, then Soweto with the revolt of a youth fired by Black Consciousness as means to freedom from spiritual dominance, then again the flare-up of organized workers' resistance, and later still a cultural revival as well, until even the whites started coming to life – and this struggle for freedom will continue way beyond the scuttling of apartheid under an ANC/NP coalition.

Reconciliation is hybridization. To the Afrikaner the implications of South Africanization will be a given loss of domination and control, to thus become an active component of a larger development; the acceptance of change, also that of self; abandoning what is perhaps the core code of Western culture, namely monotheism with its accompanying urge to convert, its fear of exclusion, the gap between what you are and what you cry out to be, utopianism, and all which flows therefrom, also in secular form, such as Marxism. But we also need to accept that transformation is an amplification and a completion, not necessarily implying radical replacement.

In the light of recent shifts in theory and practice in the country, and with special attention paid to the definition or the re-evaluation of lines of power, battlefields and zones of creativity and change, I think we Afrikaners ought to look closely at themes such as: bastardization as motivation for an intellectual, cultural and political renaissance; or a more sensitive definition of South, and an attempt to see where we fit in the Third World; from there an effort to outline our function in the South-North relationship, and therefore a theological, political, ideological and practical enquiry into the methods and contents of Africanization; and then the effort to determine the nature and trace the results of our reconciliation in such a new context; finally, to work at the critical review and evaluation, in theory and in practice, of democracy in all the segments and sediments of South African society.

An ancient Japanese poet, Daigu – meaning 'Big Fool' – wrote:

Buddha is your mind
And the Way goes nowhere.
Don't look for anything but this.
If you point your cart north
When you want to go south,
How will you arrive?

Buddha helped me understand Marx. First: there can be no Buddhism, only Buddhas. I am Buddha. And so are you, and you, and you. All of us, together or separately, are potential or actual Buddhas. Second: if you encounter Buddha, kill him! Third: my radicalism (working with or looking for roots) cannot be encapsulated in a dogma or school or party. On your own, you stepped in the dog, you yourself smelled the botheration, it is up to you to get the mess off your shoe. Four: I shall touch with my forehead the ground at your feet to salute the life and the life-carrying message in you. Five: the fact that so many people suffered for so long and sacrificed so much for the illusion of Utopia (Nirvana?) or class reprisal does not make it less of an illusion. To acquiesce to a self-denying lie doesn't make it a truth, and my esteem for smashed dreams can be shown only by highlighting them as dreams. Six: the goal can never sanctify the means; the means — this is exactly the Middle Way — constitute, every moment of the day, comprehensively the aim itself. By the way, in this resides for me the kernel of a dialectic encompassing continuous movement and engagement, for you can be neutral and unattached only if you are completely part of the process. Seven: it therefore does not mean that you can while away time in the fig-tree's shade; liberty must be realized, and this requires method, discipline, application — with the urgency of a death-struggle. Eight: the guidelines remain, even when they sound paradoxical, the solution or dissolution of self and the total respect for the Other. Nine: Let go — normally, naturally, with humour and tenderness, without clinging, not even to the letting go. Time will teach, on condition that we are ready and receptive and humble enough to learn.

I end where I started: with a call for total subversion; not for exercising an Alternative Culture, but to cultivate alternatives; not to be different, but to be — knowingly, fully, with all your aches and pains; to tie through the specific a navel-string to the universal. If we had time, we could have spoken about the law (*dhamma*) and the

Way (*tao*), and how the Law can be annulled or abrogated only by walking the Way.

Didn't Brecht argue that armed criticism can crack states? That the regulation of a river, the praising of a fig-tree, the education of a child, the reform of a state, are instances of fruitful criticism, but also examples of art?

Stellenbosch, August 1990

The Long March

from Hearth to Heart

O toi qui vas à Gao:
fais un détour par Tombouctou
murmure mon nom à mes amis
et porte-leur le salut parfumé
de l'exilé qui soupire après
le sol où résident ses amis,
sa famille, ses voisins.

These words were written by Ahmad Baba, a scholar of Islamic law, who was born in 1556 in Timbuktu and died there in 1627. During his lifetime the Moroccans laid siege to the town and conquered it, thus destroying the last Songhay empire. Ahmad Baba was accused of fomenting a rebellion against the new rulers, captured and taken in chains across the Sahara to Marrakesh, his place of exile. At the time Timbuktu was famous for its University of Sankore, and scores of other schools. Today the learning and the creation and the institutions have been swallowed by the desert, more so still by sands of neglect and indifference. From the air the town resembles a few paltry crusts of bread floating in a vast bowl of milk. Dunes silently stalk the streets and cover the walls which have taken on the colour of dead roses. A big yellow bulldozer pushes the sand from the thoroughfares in an attempt to stall oblivion. The mosque looks like the mud-drippings from a giant hand. Not far from there UNESCO subsidizes a small documentation centre where one can leaf through books such as Mahmud Kati's *Tarrikh al-Fattash* ('Chronicle of the Seeker after Knowledge') and Abd al-Rahman as-Sadi's *Tarrikh as-Sudan* ('Chronicle of the Sudan'). The oldest book dates from 1204. These volumes are kept in the open air — perhaps the fiery desert tongue preserves them naturally. An approximate translation of Ahmad Baba's words, framed in the entrance to the documentation centre, would be: 'Oh you who go to Gao, do so by way of

Timbuktu and murmur my name to my friends. Give them the fragrant greetings of an exile who sighs after the soil where his friends, his family and his neighbours reside.'

I have started at the above point because the place and its history, and the loss of its history as memory itself is sanded over, seem to illustrate one of the traits of my theme. It is not so much a rending to be separated from your own, to be rendered ineffective as it were; no, the pain is in being disconnected from normalcy and eventually becoming the living experience of the fact that exiled memory is the slow art of forgetting the colour of fire.

The theme I've been asked to talk around – it is as old as a desert map – is exile. I do so most reluctantly: I dislike the manner in which the subject has been romanticized, with the exiled ones pitied and slobbered over by vicarious voyeurs. I abhor feeding the stereotyped expectations of exile as consisting of suffering and deprivation. Those who claim to be exiles themselves only too often purvey and reinforce the hackneyed perceptions. 'Do feel sorry for us', they seem to say. 'Blame us on history. Take on the responsibility for our survival.' And for too many refugees this suspended state becomes an easy pretext for milking their hosts' sentiments. They wallow in self-pity. All experience becomes frozen. On auspicious occasions they bring forth the relics and sing the cracked songs and end up arguing like parakeets about what 'back home' was really like. They are dead survivors waiting for postcards from the realm of living. The clock has stopped once and for all, the cuckoo suffocated on some unintelligible Swiss sound, and they will continue for ever in terms of an absence which, naturally, is now embalmed and imbued with rosy dreams. They lose the language but refuse to integrate the loss, and accordingly will think less, with fewer words and only morbid references from which to suspend their thoughts. They still assume it is possible to hold back the shifting dunes of time. In the meantime the condition of exile becomes a privileged status from which, morally and emotionally, to blackmail the world with special pleading. It becomes an excuse for defeat. It is a meal ticket. And yet – isn't it true as well that exile is a chance, a break, an escape, a challenge?

I'm not suggesting that I know more or better. The fact is that I've been skirting the issue – partly because of embarrassment at the false histrionics (and I distrust my own penchant for exploiting and manipulating the situation; I, too, am attached to the familiarity of the field, as to a known insecurity), partly because it leads me to an uncomfortable self-analysis. I'm neither scholar nor theorist: what I have gleaned of the subject I can only express in elliptical or allusive terms, and often by platitude. You also become what is expected of you!

One way in which I've tried to approach the problem has been to equate exile with writing — more precisely, the creative act, because it might as well be painting. By *writing* I mean the act of using shared matter — a convention, a texture, a set of references encapsulating the codes of communication — to define or invent a history, to secrete or enshrine a viewpoint or a conduit (call it the I), and to determine a future. Different media of painting partake, for me, of different languages. The matter, or language, could after all be more or less acquired, artificial or spontaneous. Thus I always draw in Afrikaans, my mother tongue, which, because it is my mother tongue, is pre-rational. The only skill needed to draw is to sharpen the pencil. Maybe that is the only non-conditioned thinking man is capable of. I think in images and metaphors, which must complicate the communication with literal-minded people.

The individual creative act is certainly an attempt to make consciousness. This implies drawing upon memory. Memory, whether apocryphal or not, provides the feeding ground or the requisite space for the outlining of imagination. Imagination is a biological necessity for inventing a future.

The process is hazardous — but consideration such as free will, intentionality, escapism come into it, so that it can never be totally haphazard. Above all the creative act aims to be narrative. The narrative is a feint in trying to come to grips with chaos. Sometimes the only pointer is the telling. If nothing else, I am telling the telling.

From the beginning everything is. Consciously creating or 'discovering' — uncovering by chance or on purpose — implies structuring. Writing is a process and therefore a discipline. It is the discipline of using illusion by way of capturing the real. There comes a point, of course, where true reality is an illusion. You can then call it the illusion of understanding. In due time the two merge. There will be no more dichotomy, no dialectic, and finally one has death. Or one becomes death. This doesn't mean that the writing ceases. On the contrary, one accedes to the homeland of perpetual movement. In life you may be hovering on the lip of silence; in death — which is but a matter of misjudging the distance — the silence is given lips.

By the way, I recently read somewhere that Appius had expressed the wish that the letter z be banned from the alphabet, 'since, in pronouncing it, one is imitating the teeth of a dead person.' Similarly the proofreader's sign for 'delete' is a bastardized version of the Greek *thêta*, the first letter of *thanatos*, which emperors were in the habit of scribbling in the margin opposite the names of those sentenced to death.

I should perhaps have entitled my paper: From the Unconscious via the Subconscious to the Conscious, and from there to the Unconscious — and all of the above over the killing fields of reality.

I have suggested that writing is a structure for shaping experience past and present and future. It is to my mind also a means of sharpening the awareness of the interaction between the observer, or the I, and the work or the environment. Let me propose a few preliminary statements pointing at the contradictory redundancy and fertility of the state of exile: To be in exile is to be free to imagine or to dream a past and the future of that past. To be an exile is to be written.

It is hard to let go of this line of reasoning. The exile, after all, is also marked by the obsession of playing out his or her own guts. Jean Genet in his last book (*Un Captif Amoureux*), published after his death, has some remarkable passages on writing, and furthermore links that reflection to a social reality. I am translating freely and adding my own annotations: 'The Blacks in white America [Genet says] are the signs writing history; on the white page they are the ink giving it meaning.' And later: 'Translucence and whiteness [*of the page*] have a stronger reality than the signs which disfigure them ... Whiteness remains the support [*backing? environment?*] of writing, and it constitutes its margins, but the poem is composed of the absent blacks — *you may say the deads if you wish* — anonymous, the articulation of which will make up the poem whose sense will elude me, but not its realness.' Thus one may compare the written page to a white ground with black skeletons.

Roland Barthes writes: 'Life is but language.' Then he continues, rather ambiguously: 'La mort c'est l'évènement qui sort du langage.' I understand this to mean: Death is the happening — or enunciation — which flows from the language, its inevitable conclusion; or:

Death is the event outside and beyond language, and thus unspeakable.

All of the foregoing, you may have noticed, is posited on the notion of contradictions. It has been my purpose to try to reconcile the contradictions which I have experienced, to go beyond them, to dissolve them. Using exile as a *pense-bête*, I have endeavoured to make of that condition a survival technique. In other words, to wipe out oneself. One contradiction which refuses to go away is obviously that the exile cannot think her/himself loose from the process of alienation: he cannot ascertain whether what he/she has become is the natural result of ageing, whether it was exile which gave his/her tongue this bitter taste, or whether he/she used and abused this situation to become a foreigner, a *luftmensch*, in my instance a hypothetical *homo sud-africanus*. How would I have been different if it hadn't been for expatriation?

Many platitudes can be employed to describe the sharpened sense of loss and the increased awareness of gain – and I have used most of them at one time or another . . . To be away from your natural environment is to be deprived of ever again functioning completely and fitting in instinctively. No other surroundings can replace the shared and unquestioned and thereby indigenous feeling of belonging made up of smells, sounds, gestures and natural mimicry.

In the beginning there is the hearth, the ancestral fire, and you are a native of the flames. You belong there and therefore it belongs to you. Then comes exile, the break, the destitution, the initiation, the maiming which – I think – gives access to a deeper sight, provides a path into consciousness through the mimicry of thinking yourself as part of your environment. Now you can never again entirely relax the belly muscles. You learn, if you're lucky, the chameleon art of adaptation, and how to modulate your laughter. You learn to use your lips properly. Henceforth you are at home nowhere, and by that token everywhere. You learn to live with the flies, and how to slide from death into dream. You learn about creation – because you must compensate for not fitting in naturally with the environment – and thus transformation and metamorphosis, although you also come to realize that everything is since all time and creation may only be a reordering of existent images.

So you begin to understand the feel of harmony, if only because it has become a conscious construct from which you are excluded.

Therefore you acquire a knowledge of the tension between the jump or the break, and harmony, and how the one is in fact the other. You clench a fist at death. But your efforts to shake yourself free from the conventions of thinking may well, with hindsight, turn out to have been an adjustment to the harmony of dying.

You husband your weaknesses: these are the souvenirs of your native land. You make sure that you are tougher than 'they' are, or damn well learn how to pretend to be. You never quite master the mysteries of financial transactions. When you are down and out, or when your clothes are not presentable, you keep out of sight. You demand to be treated respectfully — your edges are sharper and your paranoia more acute — in fact, your evaluation of dignity becomes a taut string. You are invited to New York for a conference? Insist upon being put up in a good hotel!

You end up speaking all languages with an accent, even the distant one of your youth, the one which you kept for love and anger. You have acquired the knack of fitting in pretty much with any society; it can be said that you are a good impersonation of the cosmopolitan, but you probably never really penetrate beneath the surface of the concerns of those around you. You are engaged with an elsewhere that cannot be reached: isn't it the defining characteristic of exile?

Guard against the scratches becoming sores, the mounting tide of bitterness, the fear of losing control, the constant danger of succumbing to the shadows you see flapping their gowns at you from the corner of your eye. Remind yourself that policemen and politicians are also human.

In the book from which I have already quoted, Genet writes: 'My life was thus a composition of gestures without consequence, subtly swollen into acts of audacity. When I realized this much, that my life is written in the hollows [*engraved in counterpoint, counter acts*], this crease became as terrifying as an abyss.'

The exiled person is probably marked by a loss that he or she doesn't want to let go of, especially when occasioned by a political situation. But it goes without saying that one can replace, to all intents and purposes, the word 'exile' by refugee, misfit, outcast, outsider, expatriate, squatter, foreigner, clandestine, heretic, stranger, renegade, drifter, weakling, drop-out. The irony is that if we were to add up all these individuals we'd probably find ourselves constituting a new silent majority!

If I may at this point enter a plea of exiles at the risk of contradicting my opening paragraphs, I'd say they are often enough admirable people. The courage and perseverance, the futile quest for survival of these stowaways, wetbacks, throwbacks and other illegal humans, always astonish me: Tamils sneaking with false passports across the border, Angolans surfacing in Berlin from some 'underground railway', Ghanaians passing themselves off as citizens from Zaire or the Ivory Coast, whole families making it to the 'capital' to be crammed into one room, boat people working like beavers to build dams for a future generation. And nearly always they are starving themselves to help provide for more unfortunate relatives back home.

How resilient they are! See them come to terms with the writ of the rat. See how quickly they pick up the art of negotiating the labyrinths and warrens of Administration and Order, how rapidly they snick their tongues around the foreign language, how keen they are to learn! Along the beaches of Europe, on the squares of its cities, you come across the young men of Mali – distant descendants of Ahmad Baba – tirelessly unrolling their bundles of African kitsch made in Hong Kong, the bangles and the beads and the imitation effigies. They peddle the instantly discardable. They squint at the grey skies and wind up plastic doves which they throw in the air to flutter and fall. Somehow they survive. Have you noticed the pride and joy when these people manage to afford that first dress or leather jacket?

Still, the personal compensation of survival and existential enrichment can never justify the wilful destruction of hearth and habit, the forced removal of population groups or the expulsion of individuals. Will Romania ever recover from the mindless destruction of the peasant villages? Can South Africa knit into a serviceable national cloth the torn fibres of Apartheid? How will the Touaregs, driven to give up their nomadic existence and herded into the shallows of Western civilization, survive as fly-swatters in shanty towns? And how can one ever explain – let alone understand or condone – the crimes perpetrated by Israel when they wall up and dynamite the homes of suspect Palestinians?

My personal declaration of human rights could be resumed in four brief points: 1: Every human being has the birthright to struggle for justice and equality. 2: Every human being has the right to a home. 3: Every human being has the survivor's right to the preservation of our planet with all its life. 4: Every human being has the right to die with his or her dignity intact.

'For our purposes it matters little that strange thoughts occur to people in Albania or Burkina Faso.' This phrase from Francis Fukuyama's arrogant and fatally short-sighted article 'The End of History?' may for now seem to be apposite. Likewise Milan Kundera, in his *The Unbearable Lightness of Being*, may have been right when he chose a war in Africa during the fourteenth century as an example of the most meaningless event in human history. In proposing that any event that happens only once is meaningless, he suggests a life that disappears once and for all, that does not return, is like a shadow, without weight, dead in advance, dead by procuration and procreation; and whether it was horrible, beautiful or sublime, its horror, sublimity and beauty mean nothing. He wrote: 'We need take no more note of it than of a war between two African kingdoms in the fourteenth century, a war that alters nothing in the destiny of the world, even if a hundred thousand blacks perished in excruciating torment.' (I'm quoting from an article written by Richard Dowden in *The Independent*, 28 August 1990.) Indeed, one is tempted to ask: Why bother to look back that far? How about now?

On the continent with which I identify, whose cause — however weak — will always be mine, there are at present an estimated thirteen wars being fought: in Angola and Ethiopia and Liberia and Mali and Mauritania and Mozambique and Uganda and Rwanda and the Western Sahara and Senegal and Somalia and the Sudan and Tchad. (South Africa is not in a war situation; we just have ongoing large-scale slaughtering.) Who cares?

True, for now the rich countries or the developed world or the North — call it what you wish — evidently decided unilaterally and disdainfully that developments in the poor countries can have no incidence on the course of history (by 'developments' I mean stages of stagnation and deterioration). But this *realmoral* (the cynical underpinning of *realpolitik*) is a-historical, it brings with it a shrinking of public ethics in the rich world too. Recent events, and events to come, will show — I'm sure — that it is foolhardy for the West or the North to close its eyes and close off its heart behind the pretentious bulwarks of a 'new world order'. It was Althusser who said: 'The future lasts a long time.' History may no longer be deterministic or predictable, and it certainly does not progress, but it is never completed. It vomits at unexpected moments. I agree with Gertrude

Himmelfarb in her reading of Hegel: 'The synthesis of the preceding stage is the thesis of the present, thus setting in motion an endless dialectical cycle – and thus preserving the drama of history.'

In telescoping many contradictions and opposites, exile has provided me with a panoply of lessons. I have said that it showed me, like a flasher, the mechanisms of survival. It made my mother tongue into a 'homeland', a movable feast, indeed a dancing of the bones – as with the Famadihana ceremony on Madagascar when the remains of the deceased are brought up once a year for a festive family meal and a waltz. It gave a *taste* to words. It altered my perceptions of space and time. Time, I learned, can be stilled, warped, coloured, preserved, killed, suddenly be speeded up, and sometimes it can become immaterial. Space, I found out, can be provisional or hostile or vibrant and textured and tactile. Exile gave me motifs for my work: silence, death, transformation, shadows, ink, games, the void, dreams, immobility, interchangeability, essence, breaks . . .

It has shown me that you can become a master of dreams – since you had to recreate loss and articulate the void. I now understand that to reflect on the act of writing is to follow the courses of consciousness and not to be discoursing on the nature of the real, that it is in fact not possible to reconstruct the real as the very process of re-memberment becomes reality. I know that dreams have a meaning because their field of reference is the charted area of experience – however warped the mirror – but also that the order, the hierarchy, the linking create other references. I have learned that you can become hooked on the inner logic of dreams – and that you always become what you have mastered. I have learned that the dream constitutes a necessary make-believe, an outside border, a means of *dépassement* – and from the moment of its inception and enunciation it is a given which will modify expectations and behaviour to become a constituent element of reality. I think it has taught me something about tolerance, and that to dream, in a social sense, is an affirmation of generosity. Exile has stimulated my obsession with *métissage*, transformation, metamorphosis. Perhaps it has made me superstitious, so that I now perceive the interaction between expression or projection, and becoming or destiny. I have experienced that alienation allows one to go to the essential.

Exile has brought it home to me that I'm African. If I live in Europe most of the time, it is not as a participant but an observer, an underground activist for Africa. My pale skin and my Western garb make it possible for me to 'pass for white'. But my heart beats with the secret rhythms of that continent which seems to have sunk below the perception horizon of the North. At night I go out to scribble on the walls of the old imperial cities: *Africa lives!* In other words, I consciously try to shape my work, even the expressions of a private or peculiar idiom, as contributing to the awareness of Africa. When I'm asked what nationality I am, I say – depending on my judgement of the perceptiveness of those asking me – Brazilian, or Arab, or some impossible cross-over or quirk of displacement. Nowadays I sometimes say Canadian. Canadian sounds nice and faceless, all accent and no master text. If I were to say French or South African I would have trouble getting the worms back into the can. It is better not to drag your roots with you so as not to attract undue attention by the dust which you will raise. Roots are edible things in Africa. So is the placenta. Maybe, because of the African customs of burying the umbilical cord and eating the roots, you are in danger of becoming what you were!

Yes, exile is a difficult craft, as Nazim Hikmet imtimated – climbing up and down strange staircases. One hopes that it is also a useful one, that you may be a producer of awareness, even if marginally so. To contribute what? It is another contradiction that exile should be a pointed experience and yet, in a world of specialization, be promoting lateral vision and parallel thinking. You have to think yourself out of a hole.

Indeed, the experience and products of exile could be a dissolvent of border consciousness. It could be a way of reconnoitring, shifting and extending the limits. Somebody will remember having seen on a wall the faded subversive message: *Africa lives!* In your place of exile you would have introduced a dissonance, a feeling for the texture of awareness. And when you return to the paradise, to your native land (let us imagine it to be South Africa), it may be with scars – as Rimbaud warned – but it will also be with precious gifts: the dip and veer of swallows at nightfall over the Niger river, the depth of the seeing without judging in an old man's eyes, the fly-embroidered smile of a child, the musky woman-smell of the loquat flower. Exile teaches you about individual fate with universal implications – because it is eternal and has always been with us: we are all dimly aware of our incompleteness, of the thick veils of illusion in which we are draped.

47

Recently I went back to where the bones lie buried, and I was a stranger. My wife and I spent a night in a small-town hotel; I handed the receptionist my passport and chewed the fat with him. He congratulated me, as 'foreigner', on my ability to speak his language, Afrikaans, so well — be it, he added patronizingly, 'with an accent'. I answered that it was surely the least a visitor could do in trying to respect the customs of a strange country.

An exile never returns. 'Before' does not exist for 'them', the 'others', those who stayed behind. For 'them' it was all continuity; for you it was a fugue of disruptions. The thread is lost. The telling has shaped the story. You make your own history at the cost of not sharing theirs. The eyes, having seen too many different things, now see differently.

But the return released me from exile! The crystallized shadow was cut from me. I haven't staunched the bleeding yet, but there's hope, through mourning, of a cure. Exile became a thing outside me, which could be discarded. I wound it up and threw it in the sky to fly. I put it to earth with the navel-string, the roots and the bones.

Gilles Deleuze, the French philosopher, says in a letter written to a critic (reprinted in his recent volume, *Pourparlers*): 'Nietzsche gives you a perverse taste — that neither Marx nor Freud ever could, quite to the contrary: the desire for everybody and anybody to say simple things in his or her own name, to speak by means of emotions, intensities, experiences, experimentations. To say something in your own name is very strange, because it is not at all at the moment of taking yourself for some special I, a person or a subject, that you speak in your own voice. Rather, an individual only properly acquires his own name after a severe exercise in depersonalization, when he or she lays himself or herself open to multiplicities and the intensities which may run through him or her. The name as instantaneous appropriation of such an intensive multiplicity is at the opposite of the depersonalization affected by the history of philosophy — it is the depersonalization of love and not of submission. You speak from the bottom of what you don't know, from the cellars of your own under-development. You become — have become — a collection of singularities cut loose, of names and pronouns and fingernails and things and animals and small happenings: the opposite of a star or an expert or a preacher.'

And so I shall finish where I started — with sand and with fire. One of the pillars of Hou-neng's teaching as the sixth Zen patriarch (as if there could be pillars in the void!) was the concept of *wou-nien*. *Wou*, in Chinese terminology, is said to mean 'not to exist' or 'not to have'. The ideogram doesn't indicate 'heart', however, but literally stands for 'fire'. *Nien* signifies 'to think of', 'to remember', better still: 'present or actual thought'. *Wou-nien* is thus rendered as 'non-attachment'. I particularly like in that word-picture the sign of 'fire-consciousness'. How does flame think of itself? How does thought burn? As the fiery heart?

By *wou-nien* is the Unconscious penetrated. And where do you get the Unconscious? It is to see all things as they are and not to be attached to any of them ... It is only maintaining the perfect freedom to come and to go.

Hou-neng also consoled us with the following thought: 'You should know that, as far as the Buddha nature is concerned, there is no difference between the enlightened and the ignorant person. The only difference is that the one realizes it and the other ignores it.' Do we have a choice? Quick! Quick!

the heart of the country

we pray each day to give thanks for the sand
where we walk and sleep and which we scoop
to wash the bodies for worship –
when a prince of the capital comes to the wasteland
we prepare over the coals in the firepit a camel
crammed with a goat stuffed with pheasant
farced with a desert dove stopped with two eggs
and present the steaming fragrant caravel carcass
as if crouched for praying on the festive table –
high against the fingertips of the towers of convocation
two ostrich eggs are built into heaven
to catch and hold the full moon's light,
nothing ever decays in this burning away of time –
then we show to our guests in the holy writings
how these arabesques of the revelation of faults
like so many consonant insects of God
are silently mounted by the shifting dunes
of a timeless dream of oblivion,
and our words become sand

New York, 1990

Cadavre Exquis

The point is sharpened. Thumb and index of a hand are folded around the shaft of the pencil which fits over the middle finger. A fleshier cushion of the hand and part of a wrist rest on a sheet of white paper in order to flex the joints and their excrescence over the void. There must be unconscious concentration. From some distance above two eyes are lined up to observe this absurd contraption intended to suspend mortality. Beyond the eyes in a labyrinth where everything has existed since all time – dogs and minotaurs and lovers and emptiness and moon and handkerchiefs and blood and howling and Africa and freedom and laughing trees and eclipses and memorized imagination which is imagined memory – a form is struggling to take shape.

Form cannot exist without expression. Expression flows from movement. Movement gives birth to stillness. Stillness suggests absent movement. A line is born: the navel-string of decay written in lead. Coffins are lined with black lead, writing the environment which eventually digests the contents.

What on earth will be produced from this monstrous marriage of wood and lead and flesh and memogination? Can the eye as transmitter or transgressor retain its untaintedness and not be transmogrified? Will the howl be hanged from the rope of nothing-ness? Who is going to pay the telephone bill? Isn't the drawing a drawing of the drawing? What happened to your mother? Does Comtesse Delafesse like ice-cream? Will there be war? Did Goya eat the black sword? Read all about it in *Cadavre Exquis*! Don't miss the next instalment!

The wrist swivels to put in motion the fingers with the pencil to define immobility and thus suspend mortality. An eye is drawn, like knuckles knocking on glass. An eye for an eye. The eye looks at a hand. A hand knocks on the window-pane.

2

A hand taps on the glass. Peinêtre opens the window. Immediately the laughter of trees enters the room. The woman in the garden wears a mask and a tightly-laced bodice which leaves the backside bare. In the Bible it is written that her buttocks are brown hillocks glistening in the morning sunshine, a hive for bees and a haven for sighs. She pokes her head over the window sill.

'What are you doing?' she asks. 'Whatever it is, it must be painful. You have the furrows of sorrow.'

'Can't you see I'm drawing, dammit!'

'Ooh, you're an artist. How exciting! Or are you just unemployed and filling time? What are you drawing?'

Silence. (Except for the chuckle of leaves, the buzzing of flies.)

'Maybe the whatsit is drawing you?'

'Don't you get cheeky.' Peinêtre's hand has stopped fumbling at the paper. He looks up and puts out his tongue at her. 'You seem to forget that if I hadn't imagined you, you would not be here now to ask silly questions.'

'Why are you making so many lines?' she insists.

'Fishing for an image.' Silence, etc. Then: 'What's your name?'

'They call me Comtesse Delafesse.' She giggles and covers the mask with her hands.

Peinêtre: 'Thought so. Look, I'm probably trying to square the circle. Here I am struggling to give face to an image which I cannot know until it is revealed, and at the same time the lines are tying the picture down. The bird is trapped in the song.'

'You cannot change anything ever without yourself being changed,' she says knowingly. 'Not even silence. Only dead fish swim with the stream. And it is difficult to be in love.'

'I'm talking about birds, not fish. Look, if I draw too much I blacken the image beyond recognition.'

Comtesse Delafesse laughs. Through the window she hands him a parcel roughly wrapped in black newspaper. 'Relax,' she whispers. 'I've brought you relief. Put down your pencil and listen. Let me tell you a story.'

3

Once upon a time long ago in the distant Democratic Republic of Mirroria there lived a painter who was in search of an idea. He needed the idea to make an image or an image to draw an idea from, I don't know which and it doesn't really matter. It is an intricate process to come from nowhere. The man sat at his table and knocked his hand against his head hoping to deliver inspiration but nothing came. He knocked some more: nothing happened again. He knocked and knocked and stopped and there was the sound of knocking. He thought hey-ho it must be an angel but actually it was the postman at the door to deliver a roughly wrapped parcel addressed to one C.E. Underneath the name there was pencilled: *To lend you a hand.* Who could C.E. be? The man was suspicious of unidentified objects, he was afraid of bombs and do-it-yourself pornographic kits, he sniffed at the parcel, it smelled fishy, he chucked it into the garden dustbin. A big dog came scrounging for scraps, turned over the dustbin with a clatter and ran off with the parcel in its jaws. The man was relieved. Ah, good riddance of bad rubbish, he thought. He was afraid to give his head another knock lest the postman return and so he started to draw the parcel from memory. Someone tapped against his window. It was a masked lady with cheeky buttocks. The man eyed her bum and sighed. She handed him a parcel wrapped in black newspaper. 'I found this lying out there next to a dead dog, it is meant for you, dogs are thieves.' The man accepted the present with trembling hands, he couldn't show his fear to the lady with the brave backside, he opened it, inside there was a severed hand covered by a crust of flies. He blew over the thing, shook it, the flies weren't moved. He dumped it into a basin of water, scrubbed it, the flies stayed put. When he took it out it was white, the flies still clung to it with trembling wings, the water was red. The man looked for clues in the paper. It was a sheet from the *African News.* There was an article about an agoraphobic philosopher under the headline: *How to die in fifteen easy lessons.* Oh no, the painter thought – me and my bright ideas! Let me out! I don't know C.E. This is not for me!

4

This is not for me, Dog thinks. It is too hot, the city is too big. I'm not made for this. Noise and flies, the stench of unwashed people. Where do the flies come from? It must be all the silent screams, Dog thinks. When people open their mouths the flies just stream out, the heart must be an abattoir, flies are the visible and promiscuous dreams of poor people. There should be less talking.

To think that the poet describes the heart as the muscle of dreaming, the un-seeing inner eye. My bloody eye! To think that I came to this city of Mori to become a philosopher. What short-sightedness! Where is the mountain? To think that I was advised to look into the black mirror. What blindness! And why, pray? To fish for the image of self, Dog remembers. To plait the rope of nothing-ness from which to hang the howl, it must be said. Better not to think. (Better still not to be thought.)

Dead people are invisible. To imagine them is to make them alive, Dog thinks. He is walking the streets by day and at night, suffering from insomnia. The heat wave makes oblivion even more problematical. People look at him and open their dead fish mouths to ask: Who are you? He waves his hand at the flies. Image is illusion, Dog thinks. Image is the imitation of appearance. It is to bring to mind something which isn't there. Like thinking. The fictitious shows us the image as a drawing of an imitation which has no other reality except for its similitude with what it isn't. I've seen that things when they search for their pulse find only empti-ness and echo. Therefore thinking must be death and image its appearance. (I loved mankind so much that I sent Image, my only begotten son, to appear among you.) Therefore death is in the mind and cannot exist except by imitation. Therefore death is creation. Or initiation. If there's no death, life must be without beginning or end. Dog thinks: How can I sleep when I'm not alive?

Dream stumbles over its own reality. As the heat increases Dog the philosopher is getting thinner. He walks the streets thinking about wounded rats, wet hats, river shadows. When he returns home he looks through the small windows of his house with red-rimmed eyes. I'm looking into a dark looking-glass. Is that where I come from? What is the news? If I don't think about it, it may be alive. Mirror, mirror on the wall, who is the deadest of them all? Irritated neighbours shout: Will you shut your mad mouth?

One night he panics and starts screaming and tearing at his hair. Flies obscure the window. Dog thinks he has gone blind because it is dark outside. If I can no longer see, this dead thing is going to devour me!

5

Dear Dog,

That huge black mountain blocking out the light from your window is Africa. See? Don't let it make you despair, rather let it be food for thought. Let the mutterings of your mind wander over it like flies animating a decapitated limbless trunk. It is after all impossible to think what doesn't exist.

Imagine you are bringing to light something which already exists. To see it you must draw it, and thus you recompose the horizon. Don't do it just any old way. Better follow the road of no choices. Never let loose a dog in the bush; just now someone will start pelting you with stones. And remember that everything you will ever say may be used in evidence against you.

To imagine and to recreate already existing things, to bring back these *memento mori* from the outer rim of despair to the inner kingdom of the garden of riddles, the way I am writing you at present . . . is to establish the invisible space. Space opens vision, vision leads to otherness, otherness and space bring on relativity, relativity engenders incompleteness and thus creation, memory is the mother of creation. You can invent Death and Africa! Blindness too is a kind of seeing, and if you can no longer see, the dead thing will devour you. To see darkness is not to be blind. Darkness is just a memory of light.

Observe it then, rest your maulstick on it. Can you, as an observer watching death's walking flesh, be part of the human race? It is our madness to be simultaneously enjoying the opposites. Oh brother, since we are all guilty, it is time to change the law.

What? You hear a chanting? Close your eyes and look: isn't that a god with a cock in his arms skipping down the mountain slope? What is it you hear him saying? Africa dead? True, he is shouting in the road: 'Africa died! Africa died!' Brother, when the grave was opened nothing but silence had survived.

Don't cry. Have you not seen the miraculously yellow eyes of starving children? From the concerned regions of the world we shall export our steaks to be chewed down there and reintroduce them to our softer climes and weaker gums as digestible matter. (And we shall change the law about shouting in public.)

If you wish to forget about the problems of the disappearing image and the lost idea, draw and write! Burning is the slow art of forgetting the colour of fire. Trust the lines and the words; they know more about things than we do. Stretch the silences. Remember, a hand that writes cannot catch flies.

Together with Wadd, Zena, Peinêtre, Rehena, Comtesse Delafesse, Bogar, Angelo Mosca and Carlos Engels, I greet you.

Hétéros

6

Dead things don't bite. But sometimes they refuse to lie still. Not all of them, luckily. It would be unfair to generalize. We who are the guardians of the status quo, we'd be the first to point out how very dangerous it is to blur the borders and confuse the distinctions. In this world, in this Democratic Republic of Mirroria, from Mori in the north to Agapemone in the south every shadow has its object, every sentient being its role, each movement its weight.

But how to ensure the inviolability of the inviolate? Who will guarantee the rising of the sun at nightfall unless a virgin's chest is cut open with a glass knife to rip out a warm heart as sacrifice to that which never changes? We dare not sleep. We must struggle to preserve the balance of all the equations.

We are the executioners. Those whom we have salted away in the mud are the victims. Sometimes we must check. We go down the steps to where the heavy stone slab closes off the tomb. The warders know us. They touch the peaks of their caps with sly fingers and twirl their moustaches. We are the executioners.

We slide away the naked stone. We bend low and play the beams of our torchlights over the inner walls and the mud. There they lie, caked yellow by the mixture of clay and quicklime. Mostly they are embedded face down, draped in long travelling coats, their hair spread out in a halo made eternal by the soft decomposition of the earth.

But sometimes we catch a movement, heavy and blunt as of soaked moths. An old couple made mummies by their off-colour make-up of grime and decay are floundering and groping for one another. Are they really trying to make love? Pretending to be alive? By the light of our investigation their eyes are slowly yellow.

7

'There is nothing you can do for us, there is nothing we want from you.'

'But, Captain Wadd,' the consul splutters, 'my government has instructed me to convey our satisfaction at your terminating a corrupt regime, and to offer you our aid for democratic development.'

'*Major*', the man says. He is thin and black, his limbs slim, and his gestures — when he pours a gurgle of mint tea from a battered teapot held high above the glass — also resemble those of the locust. His cheeks are rouged. He becomes motionless.

'Major Wadd. I'm sorry, I didn't know.' The envoy is sweating in his anonymous clothes of an *éminence grise*.

'We overthrew the tyrant because he was dead —' he lifts a stick-like arm to ward off the consul's protests. 'As for your ... *support*: we know what you're really after. You want to send us your fibrous meat to masticate and return to you softened and edible. And your military attaché here, General Klebs, probably advises you to dump more obsolete jeeps and dud rockets on us, so that we may continue killing each other.'

'No, no, believe me, Major Wadd, there's a terrible misunderstanding —'

'*Colonel* Wadd to you. Don't apologize, you couldn't know. I may be weak but I'm no fool. It is not because we'll never have the power to rid ourselves of you, the albino flies, you who came here uninvited with your guilt and your greed and your pathological need to be loved, that we don't know you as intimately as if we'd drawn you. The killing? That will continue without us having to enrich your death merchants. We've done so for centuries and we shall go on for ever — with word and line and glance if needs be. You've heard what our name, *Wodaabe*, means? No? *Those who live under the taboo of purity.* One of our tribe, a philosopher, was exiled to Agapemone to purify himself from illusions. First he undertook never to use the past tense again. The past is a lie. Then he gave up laughing, because that would be to imitate trees. Then he decided to stop employing any word with an *a* in it. *A* was the beginning of *appearance*, of the rot. You know what happened to him?' Wadd takes off his sunglasses to show his kohl-rimmed yellow eyes to the red-faced consul.

'He became tongueless. He went mad. We had him evacuated to Mori. He could only whistle *The Night Journey of a Bird*.'

8

Forget about everything you have read so far. It was flyshit, the shadows of thinking, at most small clouds of graphite dirtying the paper. The communal mind is a cloaca. Forget the mind and contemplate the world. Respect what *is*. Look, everything has its place, each movement its load of weightlessness, and the hierarchy is intact: god, angel, ape, virgin, bird, man.

I am of the race of the virgins. My name is Rehena. Sometimes my wings ache for the caresses of a lover. I sit by the window and my thoughts wander over the landscape. I look for the hidden structure, that which will recompose the skyline. In the beginning one can wipe out the pencil lines with the crumbs of new wheat bread. Can whiteness be a manifestation of dirt?

I have known specimens of the inferior category of man who were white in appearance, dreaming nostalgically about dead markets where they could sell their instruments of death, of the good old times in exotic countries where hierarchy was intact and slaves could still be whipped until the flesh was purpled. I have known them to take off their glasses and caress their memories consisting of white morbific matter.

9

I sit by the window. The snowflakes softly whisper wet kisses against the glass. Maybe I shall prick my finger with a needle and a drop of blood as big as a fly in winter will stain the window sill. I'm devoured by longing, my eyes are cracked from the ravages of love. Black birds, like notes surviving a lost melody, flutter over the snowy page. And if eternity were layers upon layers of footsteps?

And totality a big white bird? I dream of clasping fire to my breasts
in the dark.

I shall travel by night, tirelessly looking for a place to die. The
sea? The boulevard? The desert? No, the mountain of fire spewing
its golden membrum virile against the night. I shall know my lover,
C.E. I want his scalding wetness to flow over me. Let it be my
moment of extinction, my *coitus eruptus.*

You will make a glass knife of my glazed corpse, to slit open the
chests of virgins so that the sun may return.

Listen, an immense howl lives inside me, a mountain. Come,
suspend your sighs from my ear.

10

you hang your sighs from my ear
the cross-examined rhythms of a shallop
I crawl into your carcass
like a mollusc in its shell
to fit in more snugly
with the shivering nightsounds of motion

the kite in heaven is a gesticulating question
as flightpath of the angel
whose answer is fed back
to the angler's hand
spelled around the motionless departure

back and back to deeper layers
of understanding your skin
is the Milky Way the unknown
unfolds before my eyes as eyes
fold in upon landscapes of remembering

11

to make love
is to go ashore
in uncharted queendoms of whistling silence
where trees spell the secret equations
of eternity

here we dwelled and here
on the flowing banks of the Ganges
where corpses hum with flies flies
like stars like darkened sacrificial blossoms
scattered over the black flow of eternity
like flies

sometimes you suspended your sighs from my ear
with the melancholy of a dancing Hungarian
back and back to the strange remembered
volutes of the shell's
white inaudibility
where we milked the light

my hand a kite
over a trajectory of ecstasy

12

This trajectory of ecstasy: what are you going on about? / Call it purification by proliferation. See this moving hand? It is making love. / And if love were but a light touch, a butterfly like a blue smile on the lips, and then the hand before the mouth to hide the worm? / True perhaps, but the lie carries within it the beginning of its own truth. / You mean transformation? / Yes, it is all a matter of shape and shape is only moulded light. / This line you're playing out, isn't it a scratch on the light? Won't it leave scars on the surface? / My dear Carlos Engels, the line is taking the place of light, you may say light is fixed by its absence. More even, the shape is a memory of light just as life is a precocious regret of death. When you leave a burning house you should take fire with you as a souvenir of safer days. / What, pray, are you drawing? / I'm drawing words. I'm in this burning house, writing a landscape to recompose the horizon. I shall evoke Goya swallowing black swords and, with tender *morbidezza*, Comtesse Delafesse smearing her mask with ice-cream and Hétéros trying to be different. / Fool! Fool! You are like Bogar the hangman peering through the peephole at the condemned creator. You are cancelling all freedom of choice. You will have a corpse on your hands. You are generating death! / When one lives in a country where people defecate standing up it is better to learn how to shit on your feet. / Don't you trust anyone at

all? / Oh sure. My pipe and ... let me think. There's my pipe and
then my shoes. They've been most faithful, even if they stink. You
see, I have never been young; I always had a headache. But don't
you go and pity me now. Even an ass can kick the dead lion. It is
better to be alive and rich than to be poor and dead. / Poor you.
Here, take this soap and wash off those flies.

13

when you are handed a bar of soap
and the warder with the fetid breath
tells you to wash your face
then it is the last night
too many expressions and gestures of loved ones
from the nothingness
the light is snow
when the hangman looks at you
through the judas-eye
then the day breaks from night's belly
and your right wrist is tied to your left ankle
and you are taken down the corridor
of lost footfalls
like a crab on a leash
already a dead hat
to the yellow room
where neither light nor sound ever penetrates
just the articulation of flies
then a white sheet and a pencil
herewith the final wordscape
the noose from the pole and the shithole in the floor
the howl dies a black flower in the mouth
oh people, death is but an anus
secreting life

14

Angelo Mosca is the perfect adjustor. One doesn't die, one adjusts
to death. And when he goes he will take his shadow with him.
Perhaps his shadow will be standing in dark places, laughing at
us ...

We all know he has been chosen to die, but he doesn't. On a bright day with wind playing like a kite among the clouds, a procession of *ad libitum* drawings accompanies him to the place of judgement. People chant rhythmically: *We want bread! We want bread!* Someone holds up a placard saying DISASTROUS. Someone else waves a sign, LOVE THY NEIGHBOURESS. Bells tinkle, banners flutter. Posters with his effigy proclaim that he was mercifully condemned to eighty years imprisonment only. We know that this is but to fool the gullible, because his death is written. Young advisors to Peinêtre are waiting at the entrance to the station. Light is putting a flare to Angelo Mosca's white penitential robe. Earnest words are exchanged . . .

He comes back to head the procession, he looks out over the distant smear of light emanating from the sea, his coffee-coloured face is serious. 'The artist is going to receive me,' he says. 'I have been promised an audition. I am his. We are one.'

I take his head in my arms and hold him tight, tight. 'Stop it!' I scream. 'You must wake up. Be yourself. You are nobody's chattel. You are free!' And I squeeze so hard trying to convey my consolation that his head comes off . . .

Now I walk forward, all the creatures following me in dense ranks, the advisors giving way. I cradle his head in my arms, blued by death. Bells tinkle, banners flap. There is a fleeting thought of blood down the front of my robe.

15

The pencil has produced the illusion of a smear of blood on the smock. Expression cannot exist without form. Maybe the accident happened when the parcel was unwrapped and the broken mirror brought to light; maybe the hand was cut.

Silence is waiting to be born. Underneath the clothes or the black newsprint or the swollen earth there is the body. Drawing is unwrapping, undoing the distance. The only line is: how to reduce the dichotomy between memory and metamorphosis, and make of the drawing a still point.

Where was I? You always draw or write a mirror. Every mirror is a self-portrait. The drawing is therefore instant memory, and the mirror a naked knife cutting the line.

Where was I? The eye peels back the black skeins over the vanity and joins limbs to trunk, it contributes golden balls to the meeting of thighs, it gives an invisible heart to a suggested outline, to the shoulders it adds a head with tongue and memory and with eyes looking at the hand: the exquisite corpse the way it is imagined by memory. Or remembered by imagination. Thumb and index of the hand are folded around the shaft of the pencil which fits over the middle finger. The point is sharpened.

Stockholm, 1991

Painting and Writing for Africa

*(on the miserable glory of creating one's own life,
the way the monkey weaves his robe)*

When I was asked to deliver a lecture at the occasion of this exhibition in Stockholm, my first impulse was to revolt against the very idea. I thought – and I still do – that it should not be necessary to talk about what ought to be a visual experience. I hoped – and I still do – that it would be possible to look, perhaps enjoy, maybe evaluate the works on show without having to know anything about the author. Not to look *through* me is the only possible way of seeing the paintings and the drawings clearly. But I also know from experience how lazy people are. We live by category, we look for explanations, our approval or disapproval is preconditioned, our faculties for direct experience are atrophied, and we mix up everything. We all have lazy and shifting visions of totality. We probably cannot hold more than one image simultaneously in the mind.

Then I realized it would be naïve and maybe even arrogant to expect that I could escape from a situation which is also of my own making. When one paints, writes, and is (or was) militantly involved in politics, it is only normal that people should want to read one activity in the light of the others. The pressure to conform by clarification is all the stronger when you are with people with whom you seemingly share a cause. You are expected to interpret, to illustrate, to bear witness. Particularly in our day and age, when what is known as the 'political discourse' has invaded the public domain to the exclusion of silence, of memory, of uncertainty, of slowness and of error. Even more particularly so in an environment of moral posturing. Never before has there been in the world such widely shared moral concern – everybody has 'human rights' on the lips – and in no other century has the human animal been so persistently cruel, destructive and barbaric to his neighbour and his environment.

63

Perhaps we have been struck with the blindness of knowing too much. We have managed to escape all responsibility and the pain of perception through the lowest common denominator of mass-engendered video illusions. We are living in the age of instant pleasure, of power intoxication, of material prosperity as the highest value, of hysterical narcissism.

For example, for a few days we have been passive participants, through the umbilical cord of the television, in the First War of the Automobile. We imbibe the lies and manipulation of information and perception, we share the vibrations of a selective indignation, we submit to the distention of ethics, we may nod agreement with a new-found pride in this proof that the West hasn't gone soft after all, that Rambo is there to kick ass and do the dirty work. When in fact it is the same old dirty war of interests, the quest for control posited on and — if I may say so — justified by an unquestioned sense of cultural superiority. It is not a war for law, morals and justice — it is sheer racism, greed and madness let loose. But we don't have to worry, we think. All we need to do to stop the war is to lean forward and switch off the television.

Please forgive me for the digressions. Naturally there are also simple human reasons for having to explain what my things are about. Talking has a therapeutic quality. It eases the tensions. It makes us, you and me, feel clever and understanding and useful and close to one another. It is like breaking bread together. Besides, and in any event, to write or to paint is to sub-contract your life. One's life is never lived in isolation. How can I reclaim my life if I keep on parcelling it out on paper and canvas? It is only normal that the 'customers' or 'onlookers' should demand access to the total picture with all its aberrations, inconsistencies and inner conflicts.

An American painter whom I admire, Philip Guston, once gave a lecture called simply: 'Philip Guston Talking'.* In it he says: 'There are people who think that painters shouldn't talk. I know people who feel that way, but that makes the painter into a sort of painting monkey.'

Raising false questions can be a way of flushing out true concerns. We who write and paint like to think that artistic imagination is a fringe activity to society, with nuisance value at best, whilst secretly believing it to be an expression of the very essence of the human

* Edited by Renée McKee, University of Minnesota, March 1979.

condition, because it is creative and transformative. We like to cultivate our difference and our differences. We know of course that everybody is different, but we are convinced that our difference is different from that of others.

Well then, I talked myself into attempting to deliver a lecture and I started jotting down some notes. In the course of these I found myself continually returning to the differences and the similarities between politics on the right hand, and painting or poetry on the left. I shall worry this bone of contention some more just now. First I want to dispose of an apparent contradiction and get my left-handed act together at least: for me writing is a continuation of painting just as painting is a prolongation of writing; I don't indulge one in the place of the other, or elucidate the one form of expression by means of the other. These two disciplines of being share the same means. You could say the three of us are sleeping in the same bed — I'm in the middle — and the blanket is too small to cover politics as well: provisionally, at least, he is staying in the dog-house.

During the writing I found myself, as often before, entangled in the expectations people may have. We all carry with us some ready-made insights, a set of mind-pictures, and it has been my experience that people get quite upset when you don't conform, when you cannot confirm their pictures or their desires. When you are perceived as a spokesman or a witness you may sense the pressure of people who want you to say what they expect to hear, or what they imagine that they would have said and done had they been in your situation. This, by the way, is one of the strains in the make-up of the intellectual's guilty conscience.

In my case (and forgive me for the caricature or the unsolicited paranoia) I have the impression that people are waving their fists and shouting: 'Tell us about exile! Give us, again and again, the juice extracted from your years in prison! Confirm for us that Afrikaans is a racist language and that the Boere are all fascists! Make us feel sorry for you! Agree with us that it is a manifestation of Euro-centrist insensitivity to demand a clearness and honesty of mind and morals in those who have been exploited and oppressed! Give us politics, none of your confusing and ambiguous artistic prattling! Agree with us that we are on the right side so that we can all be uplifted together!'

Art is about awareness and about communication. To be alert to the listener or for that matter to the person speaking to me, I find that one has to talk *against* the conventions and the perceived expectations. Maybe you never *create* anything. Maybe you can only help uncover the deadened feeling of being alive by peeling the eye and stripping away certainties. In other words, if I don't just want to do the mumbo-jumbo, if I want to make you aware of the texture of what I'm saying, then I have to talk against the grain.

I call these notes, which are neither manifesto nor confession, 'Painting and Writing for Africa'. To say in Afrikaans that something is 'for Africa' means that there is a lot of it, an abundance, perhaps an excess. Thus, now that we are about to celebrate the 200th anniversary of his passing away, one could say: 'Mozart wrote music for Africa'. Or, to be somewhat morbid: 'A few days after the horse died its carcass was infested with maggots for Africa', meaning there were thousands of them, like bureaucrats around the State. Or, to home in on present events: 'Gorbachev has dispatched soldiers for Africa to the Baltic States.' Or: 'The crusaders for democracy are at this moment dropping bombs for Africa on Baghdad'. Or: 'Black people in South Africa are killing one another for Africa.' You will appreciate that it is unfortunately not possible to say now: 'In Ethiopia and Sudan and Mozambique there is food for Africa.' Even less: 'The young Africans have promises and expectations of a future for Africa.'

Although there are some people who tell me I've been wasting my time these past years trying to do what others were doing so much better, namely flogging political ideas and moral positions when I should have been painting and writing, I still think I have produced far too much. Sometimes I feel like I'm being engulfed by my own secretions. My excuse would be: I try to live by what I make. We all know that it is getting harder to survive. The less I sell the more I have to take out and show, and paintings and poems are unfortunately not self-destroying like military hardware. Had that been the case I could have said: All I need is a good war. In fact I live on advances from my publishers which they never recover. Anyway, this exuberant production, not to call it verbosity or a diarrhoea of images, would be the first connotation of my talk's title.

The second echo is also related to Africa. When you are poor and desperate and without faith or hope, why not paint and write? Many poor people in Africa are involved in the futile pastime of making knick-knacks, derisively grimacing at the unknown. The positive side to this is that people are not attached to what they bring forth. Allow me to generalize: Africans are not very talented at being bourgeois. True, we also prance and show off with our eye-blinding watches, our Gucci shoes and our ridiculously dressed-up presidential guards, and protocol is damn serious business – indeed, the less power we have the more we enlist pomp and ceremony; you may say we march with wooden Kalashnikovs for Africa – but by and large Africans are poor merchants. That may be one reason why the continent has to look North for survival, why we are all living from someone else's hand to the hungry indigenous mouth, from hand-outs and advances which the donors will never recover. Africa is in the paradoxical situation of being one of the oldest civilizations continuously having to invent itself. Could it be because the criteria of recognition are Western, and that Africa is always living below the horizon of historical perception, and sinking fast? Africa is getting to be so dark that we no longer see it. Africa, it would seem, does not make history. History is a Western way of digesting time; it is a White man's burden.

So why not paint and write against oblivion and extinction? This implies that the things thus fashioned are free, of little political or material interest, and meant to be enjoyed. Indeed, in presenting these works to you (more precisely, these workings) I hope to have you share in the joy I experienced when making them. They are certainly not intended to transmit guilt, or a message or some late post-modernist truth; if anything, I wanted them to flesh out the nakedness of being by way of exploring and, ideally, extending consciousness, a joyful pilgrim's guide along the miserable road from the agony of birth to the obscenity of death.

A third possible meaning of the title I have already hinted at, and that is that I shall go down with SS Africa, this sinking continent. I can't see myself joining the Western alliance. More precisely: since the trees have disappeared I shall continue flying, pretending that one doesn't need a place to roost or rest. Let this flight and this song then be a love-token to Africa, a contribution to the ongoing, perhaps self-defeating process of inventing an identity. When you are nothing and have nothing, you have to invent yourself. (Or you have only yourself to invent.) This bringing about is a transforma-tion, a bastardization. It is the joyful despair of metamorphosis. It is also the invention (and inventory) of nothing. Paintings, writing poetry – these are acts of appropriation. All is highway robbery. You become who and what you paint and in the process you may well lose yourself, your point of departure. You establish your own family of birds, horses, apes, people, painters and flowers. You steal the light by multiplying the images. In return you give neither cryptograms nor coded messages, but a story which will be unique and different for each person coming into contact with it.

Allow me to free the mind further by suggesting that creating is a coming to grips with death through the illusion of life. Africans, Asians and Arabs may not be in the position to outlive the West, but they are certainly much better at dying than the Whites are. Creation is the making of death. I'm not going to elaborate any further on this except to say that to my mind there's a difference between exploring the void and adding to the emptiness.

Every painting, drawing or poem is a landscape. Or a mindscape. It constitutes a location and a situation in the same way that a landscape does. Perhaps the very notion of 'landscape' is a projection of an acquired experience. Do we not, consciously or unconsciously, 'see' the landscape as a defined, even an enclosed experience? Like a painting? Similarly each is a portrait in that it portrays the combination of the familiar with the unfamiliar that we find when we gaze upon a face. In a face the eyes, nose, mouth and ears establish the immediately recognizable familiarity, the handholds for the eye, you may say, the political doctrine, that which can guide you into the unknown.

Every portrait – landscape or poem or other depiction – is a self-portrait. This is so because depiction is recognition and exposition. You may recognize what had been assimilated, that which is now part of you. By exposing a vision you are making it part of you – a light feeling like a shadow. You are the maker and the giver. You can only make *with* or *from* yourself and you can only give *of* yourself.

Every portrait is also an ancestor. (This should illustrate the title of my exhibition here: 'Self-portraits and other ancestors.') Not only because of what I have just tried to establish, but also because you are modified if not born by your own making. To put it differently: you apprehend what you see or experience (and memory is also an experience) by means of what you already have, and this act of apprehension or incorporation will change you, will add on to you.

Consciousness is the go-between, the begetter, and the matter of consciousness is image or metaphor.

The image need not be figurative to be an agent of transformation, but it will always be a configuration of its constituent parts — colours, rhythms, shapes, textures — so whether we look at an abstract painting or a concrete poem, we are seeing a 'figure'. Another way of putting it will be: there is no *I*, just a series of temporary jottings, a brief bundling of being which will delineate as if along a dotted line the passage of an I (eye), an ancestor, a mask.

The human would seem the only animal born with the memory of death, or the imagination thereof. For that matter, isn't memory imagination? And imagination of that which is conceivable? The echoes of destruction must have occupied the minds of men and women through the ages. We ourselves are the thoughts, the projections and the resonances of destruction. And yet, thinking also always moves within the horizons of one's own times. Ours have been particularly contradictory: soaked in blood, and with an increased concern for life; killing the environment, and fired by green thoughts; cheapening human interaction by communication media, and making information more democratically available; the implosion of utopia, and the resurgent awareness of the need to dream; the slackening of public mores, and the rise of fundamentalist puritanism. We need to think again the limits of our thinking.

Is it possible to be confronted by the image without the intermediary of thought? Image partakes of memory and imagination, of hollows and shadows. And thought? Can we see clearly? Perhaps all thinking is a series of concessions, of shaping the mind to attempt the interplay between the arbitrariness of convention and the fresh pain of unfettered perception. Image, I said, is the matter of consciousness. But consciousness is of course not pure or autonomous; it is conditioned to want to 'understand' immediately. Maybe 'understanding' is only situating.

The paintings and drawings I have on show here are not documents, they are images. It follows that images can be interrogated: what do they speak of? Where do they come from? What is their history? Whom do they speak to? How do they speak? Each of these questions dovetails into a series of reflections — the contents, the history, the social context, the means. But not the *meaning*. First of all, and also in the final instance, I believe it is the primary function of the painter or the poet to present an image. To present an opinion would be authoritarian. Similarly I believe the primary confrontation to be between the viewer or the reader and the image presented, face to face as it were, with neither intermediary nor a priori.

The painting as anonymous or masked messenger, as a reflection of breathing, a continuous shaping of consciousness, can be a weapon also. Let me explain. If you can *look* without projecting *a meaning*, you will be confronted head-on by an embodiment of being. 'Meaning', 'understanding' — these neutralized the threat of the unknown or the unexpected. After all, you can control meaning, but you cannot regiment seeing. Thus the instant relationship between the viewer and the image (and the one is inexistent without the other) is an uncontrollable expression of freedom, ideally the establishment of a free zone not embattled by convention or by fashion, but also one of confrontation. To sum up: when the mind has no meaning, seeing becomes a weapon for liberation.

A painting, like any other fulcrum of existence, is at the same time both frozen and fluid. It is a mess of many parts. To quote Philip Guston once more: 'People ask me what emotion a particular work is intended to convey, what emotion or sentiment went into the making — I answer . . . bits and pieces, including pure hazard.' And it is true, you cannot hold any one emotion for the length of time it takes to make a painting. We are involved in an elaborate game. The words in a poem, the marrying of light and absence on the flat surface of the painting or the drawing — these can never have one unique and unchanging meaning. Guston says: 'I don't know what a painting is; who knows what sets off even the desire to paint? It might be things, thoughts, a memory, sensations, which have nothing to do directly with painting itself. They can come from anything and anywhere, a trifle, some detail observed, wondered about and, naturally, from the previous painting . . . It moves in a mind . . . It is an illusion, a piece of magic, so what you see is not what you see . . .'

A word of caution may not be out of place here. 'Meaning' is mystery. I don't say it is mysterious; I'm suggesting that it is impossible to convey meaning because it is something which must be experienced. Experience *is*: it cannot be described. Description is, in and of itself, *another* experience. The more you attempt to describe it, the more you isolate (and perhaps identify) the indescribable. I am not religious, but I can see the uses of theology and the interpretation of texts: you have to keep on splitting hairs to make sure that God doesn't lose his face, doesn't fade away. If you were to stop laying down the traps and the nets of explanation, you may well become God – and then, where is your God going to be? We must talk because we cannot know. Maybe we talk in order not to know.

At this point the patient onlooker or listener would probably want to say: 'But brother, there is nothing particularly African in what you bring us!' This, ladies and gentlemen of the court, would be my defence: the vehicles of creation, the formal restrictions and characteristics, the possibilities and the impediments and the hesitations, are the same in all cultures and since all time. But now, faced by the New World Order and pushed to the outer limits of madness, every modern painter and poet has become an African – in that we are involved in creativity as a disappearing act.

These notes turned out to be longer and more obscure than I intended them to be. To finish more or less where I started, let me return to the differences and the links between politics and image-making. I'm through with politics. Not that I was ever tempted to become a politician. But I participated and tried to use political thoughts and language. I believe it is necessary to thus exercise publicly a commitment to civic responsibility. I have spoken here and there on the evils of Apartheid and the need to resist exploitation; I participated in conferences on racism; I even imagined some myself, trying to erect culture against barbarism; I wrote inflamed essays and then came away with a glow of satisfaction. But then, bit by bit, came the slower fire of the gangrene of the mind, of the tongue giving the taste of ash in the mouth.

The most obvious trap in which I'd fallen again and again was: to tell people what they wanted to hear, and then to be flattered by their admiration. The first one covered a second more vicious trap: that I was capable of clear analysis and original insights in the murky struggle for freedom, and that my voice was therefore *necessary*. Underneath that a third: in doing so at the expense of doubt-filled painting and writing I made myself believe that I was bringing the self as sacrifice, and thus establishing an admirable example of self-denial.

In politics there can be no reality, only an interpretation of reality. I found political thinking posited on the need to manœuvre ideas and projections. Perhaps because it moves from the assumption that the lever which puts human affairs in motion is power – its nature, who should have it, to do what with, and above all how to get it. For the power player everything flows from this starting-point. Thinking is action with the purpose of obtaining power, and for obvious reasons the way there is paved with manipulations and lies.

I found political language not only sterile but sterilizing. At times it is a dour art form in itself, with its own codes and effects and flourishes of rhetoric. But it is never self-doubting, dark or broken. It cauterizes the running sores of words, it stultifies the unexpected and unpredictable vitality that may erupt from rhythms and images and silences or a combination of these. It brings down the bird of fancy. To the writer the use of political non-thinking and of prattling by rote is fatal – because these generate a taste of disgust with words and with thoughts. The exercise of politics, it would seem, makes it impossible to be humble, available and understanding, to put yourself in the posture of listening to the unheard – the crackling of stars perhaps, or the whisper of grass.

Why did people want to listen to me? Fool that I am, I thought it was because they admired the thought. In reality it must have been because I comforted the prejudices and the stereotypes, thus partici-pating in spreading the spartan voluptuousness of having a good conscience. Maybe people were titillated or impressed to see a White taking up the cudgels for the Blacks. If that was so, then it confirms the sclerotic thinking or the convoluted racism in the minds of the listeners.

I know of no political system that has made being born worth-while or dying any easier.

And yet, I hasten to add that I don't regret any of my commit-ments. This much ought to be clear: the status or the function of the artist in society never can exculpate him or her from the responsibil-ity – and the privilege – of combating injustice. He or she has the same rights and duties as the banker or the cobbler. There are times when the struggle must be political and armed to be effective. If I had to I'd do it all over again, I know which side I'm on, and if I could undermine the rich and the powerful – the bankers, the rulers, the secret police, the tax collectors, the television journalists, the popes and the arms merchants and the Swiss and the Americans – I'd do so in all the possible ways.

But this time around there'd be no holds barred for me, I'd not be holding back my tongue for fear of rocking the boat, I'd not let myself be bamboozled by sly arguments on 'strategy' and 'tactics'. There'd be no special pleading and no moral blackmail and no dependance on hand-outs.

It is at this underground level — linked to the subterranean continent of Africa, with the I at best a displaced image, a trapped shadow fixed and waiting to be revived — that artistic creativity and politics are bonded. Both can be agents of awareness, of transformation and bastardization. It can be the same search for putting in motion the joyful despair of metamorphosis. On condition that it be subversive, existential, and without interest or gain.

Stockholm, 1991

An Open Letter to Nelson Mandela

Cape Town, 16 April 1991

Dear Mr Mandela,

Allow me to be so presumptuous as to address this open letter to you. It may be seen as a dog barking at the passing caravan — I can't pretend to fully understand the complexities of the present situation, and my reading is prejudiced, and a letter is a poor substitute for helping to staunch the spurting wounds of our society — but everything possible must be done to alert as many people as can be reached to the consequences of state and communal violence. From the poor man's Beirut in the Reef townships to the mindless mayhem in the Cape's squatter camps to the killing fields of Natal and the much bigger explosion looming in the Eastern Cape, this country is at the point of tearing itself apart.

Many anguished voices have cried out to warn that no political motive, no strategic advantage, no cause and no struggle can justify our cynical indifference to the issue of death. The killing is not just mortgaging the attempts to negotiate a different kind of South Africa; it is rotting society with its wake of corruption and revenge and bestiality, and we are all being progressively brutalized and driven down the road towards the abattoir of a repressive State.

Now the ANC, by your hand, has finally and belatedly spoken out, making future negotiations dependent upon a resolution of the violence. It is good that you recognized the urgency. Indeed, you, Sir, would have had no further national role to play unless you were seen to be responsive to the agony of the population, and perceived to be effectively leading the ANC out of this vicious circle of fire.

I notice that the Government and those media which have always been white-skinned about black death maliciously interpreted your letter as an admission of weakness, the result of internal strife, a stalling technique. It was to be foreseen that they would do so, and under other circumstances these would have been justified perceptions of the ANC's troubles. But they refused to read the reason for

74

your letter: that nothing can be solved until the killing spawned by poverty and the passion of hatred – and feeding these – is stopped.

I have just returned from spending a few days in the Midlands region of Natal. I was taken for a drive through Kloof along the most expensive properties in South Africa, a veritable paradise for the white rich on the heights above Durban. Purple-flowered shrubs and palms and all manner of tropical vegetation showed the silver and green colours of money. It is said that these lushly shaded mansions, out of this world as it were, are guarded by specially trained young Germans. Then, within a stone's throw, as we dipped over the crest, we came to where the earth fell away over rolling hills clotted with the shacks of rural Kwazulu's poverty. Cattle wandered over the road, young unemployed men lolled against the wall of a rare dilapidated general store, kids were trekking back from school down the valley. The splendid isolation of colonial luxury and the desperate isolation of black holes, the First World and the raw futility of a miserable subsistence living cheek by jowl.

More: this was a war zone, the visual manifestation of the heart of violence. With the naked eye one can judge where 'Comrade land' ends and 'Inkatha land' begins. On the one side the wasteland of roofless houses and burnt-out schools (their inhabitants now refugees elsewhere), on the other (of the same community) the maize patches and mango trees of areas where the rule of warlords holds sway. It was explained to me how one could sit on the privileged heights in a grandstand position and watch the Inkatha impis sweep down to 'clear out' the Christian or communist or trade union or civic or teachers' or students' association 'scum'. Kombis (small buses) transporting firearms would speed along the ranks to deliver and recuperate the instruments of killing. A helicopter with Chief Minister Buthelezi and Law and Order Minister Vlok aboard would whirr above the battlefield. 'Bring me the evidence,' Vlok would later say. And: 'The ANC is the common denominator to all violence.'

Again and again I was given graphic descriptions of police collusion. A warlord would at last be charged with multiple murder, his docket would be 'misplaced', necessitating a postponement of the trial, and the witness would be killed before the case could resume. In Harry Gwala's* office, he of the paralysed arms, I met

---

* Harry Gwala is the ANC leader of the Natal Midlands Region.

people who'd just escaped a third assassination attempt by hit squads. I listened to the shrill tone in the voices of the survivors and the body-counters, those who get drunk and laugh in the way only the bomb-shocked do. I learned that only the physical presence of a few concerned whites in the townships can prevent the police from initiating, aiding and abetting the killing.

The ANC has been outmanœuvred by the State. A senior Government minister remarks to me that, in their view, there is a vacuum below the top leadership of the ANC and people lower down are only interested in making money. It must mean that the Government has tried and is trying to co-opt you, thus hoping to split you from your followers. It is blackmailing you by locking you into the 'objective conditions' of collaboration. A 'new South Africa' is dangled before your nose, and the State President obstinately refuses to admit to the intrinsically criminal nature of the Apartheid state and culture which he is trying to rescue by dint of reform and international acceptance.

Can one blame him when 'the enemy', the ANC, is so weak? You would lose nothing but dead illusions if you were to point out that the ANC is victim of its own propaganda and the creation of myths and aspirations that could never be satisfied – such as, that there was an 'armed struggle', that the 'necklace'* could be a tool for liberation; that the whites could be prevailed upon to 'hand over power'; that the world worries about our plight and that it owes us solidarity; that that which has died the death of ignominious conceptual and structural failure in Eastern Europe can be resuscitated here. We must own up to the unpleasant recognition that the ANC is not (yet) a democratic organization, that it still shows a hegemonistic drive based on intimidation, that it was never a vector for revolution. The ANC is a resistance movement fashioned from the suffering of generations, embodying the search for justice of a people, the only organization capable of preserving and perhaps realizing the dream of South Africanness. And it is in the process of feeling (and sometimes fiddling) its way to becoming a responsible political structure. You must show us the way, Sir, by admitting that it is now counter-productive to be plaintively insisting upon sanctions in a world suffering from historical memory loss and a

* A tyre soaked in petrol, put around the victim's neck and shoulders, and then ignited.

recrudescent racism, where money will always flow to where there can be exploitation. Why should we maintain the fiction and the absurdity of a cultural boycott which has seen the empowerment of mediocre cultural commissars and would-be impresarios?

We must all break loose from the ban of a culture of 'security', clandestinity, secret brotherhoods and cabals, manipulation, arbitrariness, intimidation, co-optation, élitism, indifferencè to human life and dignity ... The Government must not be given reason to believe that you are like them. To enter into their cynical games is to betray your heart and deaden your tongue.

Somehow we must all inspire and articulate the national will: to stop the violence, to become productive and autonomous so that we may be freed from the humiliation of hand-outs, to change those economic structures which are the result and the beneficiaries of Apartheid and thus to start narrowing the gap between the starving and the stuffed, to create the conditions for democracy, to lay the foundations for a society in which we can take pride. That, to my belief and satisfaction, is what the ANC's constitutional proposals are pointing towards.

There must be local and regional and national elections, there must be an elected constituent assembly, there must meanwhile be a caretaking neutral authority — an interim government or some form of international supervision. And all this can only come about through sustained popular mobilization and participation (but let's please ban that disdainful nineteenth-century terminology of 'masses'!), and through brave and visionary leadership.

You may well ask why I didn't write this letter to President De Klerk? It is my conviction that we are still living through the planned horrors of the Apartheid state in its death throes, with skilled and motivated agents in the State apparatus practising a scorched earth policy in moral, political and human terms. I have no doubt that this present dissolution was programmed: judiciously controlling resources, profiting from a modified world environment, destabilizing the population, vying for hypocritical 'respectability' and bogus 'moral high grounds' (*that* coming from national death masters!), dragging out the process — in the hope that the ANC would crack in the 'African way' along ethnic lines, its spine broken by internal contradictions and the weight of popular expectations. President De Klerk is in the hands of the monsters created by a totalitarian, profoundly immoral state.

It is my conviction that the war never stopped. For the authorities, 'negotiations' were a means of continuing the war of attrition against the population of South Africa. I also believe that there was never a 'Third Force'. From the outset Inkatha was intended as a national vigilante force. Now the Government Broeders* have stretched out red hands to take the hand of Buthelezi — slippery with blood and crocodile tears — to hoist him to a position of national eminence.

Yes, the Government may well win this war in the short term, wheeling out its Parliamentary Forum and joining with Inkatha and dissident or corrupt black community leaders. They may destroy, as in Mozambique, Angola and Namibia, but ultimately they cannot construct. They cannot win the peace. They cannot rule against the majority and it is foolish for them to bargain on the ANC splitting. Their 'victory' will be pyrrhic, propagating the seeds of South Africa's final demise.

It is the tightening of the heart, it is the vision of this death-in-waiting, Sir, that permitted me to write to you, to join my voice to those weeping in the townships. And to reaffirm, come what may, that your cause is mine also. If only you will lead.

With fraternal respect.

NOTE

My open letter of April 1991 — and a public response by Chief Gatsha Mangosuthu Buthelezi (of pained surprise that I, an old friend, should thus publicly and ignorantly take sides against him and Inkatha: a not unreasonable reproach) — got some attention in European newspapers. It was also the subject of a report by the French ambassador in Pretoria to the Quai d'Orsay. Early in June, Nelson Mandela arrived for a visit to the French capital. Mischievous officials wanting to hedge their bets, or trying to obtain some influence over the negotiations then taking place in South Africa, confronted the ANC leader with sceptical questions. They referred to my letter as argument. The problem was that Mandela had never read the letter, although it had been published by the largest Sunday newspaper, eliciting the reaction of his arch rival! (Which goes to show how his entourage filtered his access to information.)

* Members of the Broederbond (League of Brothers), a semi-secret 'cultural' organization of white Afrikaner males in power. It operates as a think tank and a controller of power behind the scenes.

So he called me late on the evening of his first day in Paris to ask what it was all about. I took him a copy early the next morning with an enclosed private letter which, in part, went as follows:

Paris, 5 June 1991

Some time ago I had the cheek to write an open letter addressed to you; I don't know if you saw it published in the *Sunday Times*, and if you did I hope you didn't take it amiss. A second article has since been published, very critical of the ANC, and perhaps unduly sombre about the future. My criticism and my apprehensions may seem too exaggerated: they flow from a personal reading with its blind spots and hopefully a few insights. I'm aware that pessimism may not always be expressed at the right moment, and may be misused by our adversaries. Those are some of the risks when one works as an individualist. But the situation at home is desperate and I'd like you to know that my dissent, even when it is too harsh or unfair, is always meant as a manifestation of critical loyalty. I believe in the cause of the ANC. I believe that I owe it to my convictions to say things as I see them, and I truly hope they are accepted in that spirit. (Please do not think that I consider my remarks or observations that important, though!)

Anyway, after that open letter a friend took me to task for 'summoning' you to lead (and saying that I endorse your cause, which is our shared struggle) without suggesting what ought to be done. His arrow hit home. And although it would be ludicrous for me to pretend to suggest policies or to prescribe attitudes, I thought it would only be fair to specify my thinking some more. The remarks I'd like to submit to you have as much to do with perception as with substance, and — written in a hurry — will be disordered in that they mix short-term and long-term goals. Again: my point of departure is a belief in the justness of the ANC's cause; I believe in fact that the ANC should show far more confidence in the historical correctness of its struggle so that it could afford to be far more supple and less paranoid, and also because in an old-fashioned way I believe that unity is forged in action (that is, that you could show stronger visionary leadership to *pull* people with you), and finally that it is *urgent for the ANC to regain the initiative.*

1. I agree with the creation of self-defence units; these are the

minimum measures of protection that need to be taken. They are not going to stop the killing. I think it would help if sympathetic whites – not ANC members – could be persuaded to take turns in spending time in the townships, so that there will always be numbers of neutral whites present, day and night.

2. Similarly, I believe it is high time to invite in representatives of foreign NGOs, to monitor the situation and to interpose themselves between the warring parties.

3. The ANC needs to impose far more discipline on their own members, to convince them to refrain from intimidating people (and more disastrously, the press!).

4. It is incumbent upon the ANC to clarify and sort out its internal alliances. It is nonsense to pretend that one could hold high office both in the ANC and the South African Communist Party – nobody is fooled and the historical reasons no longer wash. Credibility will be gained, the ongoing debate clarified and the alliance strengthened if the persons involved were to assume their convictions and differences clearly. How else are you ever going to go to the polls, for instance?

5. The ANC should propose the creation of a permanent forum grouping as many political (and trade union and civic) formations as possible – all those committed to the fleshing out of an 'alternative' South Africa. The idea is to promote the discussion of all the issues, to arrive at some shared decisions on principles and projects which will be *democratically binding* on all parties participating. I am obviously here not referring to the National Party – the only way to help De Klerk along is to isolate him and to oppose him vigorously. But it is essential for the ANC to show itself capable of co-operating loyally with groups which do not fall normally within its orbit (the Democratic Party, for example), and to stop manipulating 'fronts' or 'allies' through 'plants' or whatever. Most of the white intellectuals, for instance the Dakarites* and other sympathizers (and the same goes for Black consciousness adherents), have been left out on a limb, cold-shouldered, neglected arrogantly, so that many of them are now falling in with the present regime.

6. Which is why I believe it necessary to initiate and promote

---

* Progressive South Africans who had travelled to Dakar in Senegal in 1987 to meet with the ANC, then still banned and exiled.

discussion and research groups, sector by sector covering all disciplines and walks of our community life — to contribute thinking and planning towards a new vision of our nation. It is *urgent* that the ANC should be seen to be promoting the involvement of *all* South Africans, in terms of their concerns and knowledge and interests, in a non-sectarian way. South Africa is not going to be shaped by the ANC only, and it is not the exclusive concern of the 'leaders' and the élite. We have to break the horrible culture of co-optation.

7. In the name of common sense and generosity, and as an act of faith in its own justness, the ANC should do away with the redundant policy of advocating sanctions. Similarly, it is time for us to break out of our beggar attitude of dependancy on the outside world. Stop being the victims. The ANC is not the aggrieved party, but the actors for change and construction, taking and transforming the means at hand. The resources are at home.

8. Finally, it is my conviction that far more attention should be paid to the cultural sector. That is where, in a creative richness of diversity of origins and expressions, the notion and the awareness of a national identity will be shaped.

Please accept the expression of my sincere good wishes, and do forgive me my impertinence.

An Open Letter to Nelson Mandela

Berlin, 17 May 1994

Dear Mr President,

'The time to build is upon us,' you announced only a few days ago when you were being sworn in as President of South Africa. Although your speechwriter had obviously plundered the archives of our century's kitsch calls and hack phrases in order to pluck every conceivable string, it was the noble thoughts that shone through your address. It may be presumptious and indecorous of me to write to you like this while the champagne is still bubbling; I do so because I want to endorse those sentiments.

I do so also on the understanding that you want all of us to participate in the scaffolding of a different tower of Babel. I welcome the invitation and should like to take you at your word. Please accept it as the mark of respect I intend when I say my collaboration will be conditional and critical.

Like millions the world over I watched your performance – with a certain soreness of the heart for not being in the country and with a spate of private emotions and public pride tumbling through the mind. You looked so solemn standing there clutching your heart (why this American gesture?), and while your daughter in red obviously knew even the words of 'Die Stem', your lips didn't move for either anthem. Maybe you don't have to sing any more. I urge you to continue, even if only to exercise your breathing. But then, it also looked as if you were hearkening to some inner voice.

A lady called from Amsterdam to say she'd been too young to be transformed by Kennedy's death, but this time she knew she was witnessing history in the making.

Thus our lives are touched. Quotes and snippets surfaced. Such as: 'Freedom is just another word for nothing left to lose'. Or an old Mexican saying: 'He whom the gods don't like they make one of them'. Or: 'Understanding is the process of giving meaning to suffering'. Or (from Antoine de Saint-Exupéry): 'Perhaps the goal doesn't mean anything, but the getting there delivers us from death'.

Rest assured, Mr President, it is as a fellow human being that I respect you, not as some African fetish. You are but the first among equals, facing like all of us the grinning mask of death, that ultimate macho pig. And the time will come only too soon (it always does) for would-be successors to scrabble and scratch over the spoils and to brandish your mummy as an effigy of legitimacy.

There had been silences in the text of transition, to put it mildly. (And the subtext was rather red and sticky.) The elections as a founding statement of shared dignity had gone far better than expected, even though marred by fraud and fumbling of historical proportions. Naturally the politicians promptly tried to take back the people's voices by manipulation and interpretation. Most important – the violence has apparently abated. (If there's a link between effect and cause, why can't we vote every week?) So far the doom prophets, including yours truly, got it all wrong (or is it just that South Africa has fallen off the front pages of the international media?), and how wonderful it is to be wrong!

The euphoria will however not last. People may be patient, but patience is neither food nor shelter. And so we are called upon to channel the discrepancies and to build a nation. In other words, we have to imagine the syntax of reconciliation, this process of bonding around mutually understood notions and shared values. Perhaps even with symbols we can all make our own – and the first of these, the new flag, is such a disastrously ugly flop! We have to invent that harmony which consists of dynamic change. We have to invent ourselves.

Some of your first steps were not encouraging. Your choice of ministers, please permit me the remark, was superbly unimaginative. Inevitably, one accepts, it had to be a *lappieskombers* (a patchwork quilt) of divergent interests that had to be stitched together. But did you have to include quite that many crooks and demagogues and dogmatists? Among those smooth misters and madams are people with blood on their hands (or, at the very least, who ought to have blood on their consciences). One could say, well yes, but it's still better than the previous bunch of liars, thieves and moral amnesiacs. Too true. But not good enough as an excuse, given the wealth of qualified and committed South Africans you could have called upon.

You have decided, practically by presidential decree, that there are no more barbarians gnawing at the frontiers of enlightened decency. ('Those people were a kind of solution' – Cavafy.) Even so, national reconciliation is not just an order or a pious wish. It must be a sustained process. We South Africans have not experienced the historical purge of a revolution (not yet at least, and if it does occur it will be hell let loose), but if we were to move decisively along the road to a creative blending of energies we may still accomplish a revolution of our very own which could conceivably open the way to the treatment of our urgent social and economic problems.

In this great leap forward to bring about democracy with a human face we shall have to be inspired by the many paradoxes inherent in our society. People who are strong, maybe even forceful, in their differences are the ones who fit in easier with a more comprehensive grouping. The cultural reflection around the dialectics of tribal and national identities is going to be primordial. Fascism, in cultural terms, is the imposition of grandiose and formalist schemes which in the name of patriotism and justice allow for neither evolution nor innovation, immaterial whether the justification used is of liberal or socialist inspiration. I take it you want us to avoid this drift to self-congratulatory totalitarianism.

Unless governance is to be an unending play of power moves behind closed doors, erupting on the streets from time to time in the ploy of 'mass action', we have to become actively tolerant of diversity in order to assure movement. Too strong a concentration of power will itself be an impediment to moving forward.

You know (and what has been inflicted upon you proves the point) that we have no such tradition of tolerance or common sense. The National Party did not set out to dismantle Apartheid (which, from the oppressors' point of view, had been vastly success-ful, enriching generations of whites while weakening their moral fibre to the point where they became estranged from simple truths) because of a conversion of heart, but because they were manœuvred into submission by a combination of factors. Similarly big business, which could play such a powerful role for change, will never relent in its unslakeable thirst for ever bigger profits until obliged to do so. Only the overtly racist half of the Apartheid beast is dead; the other half, economic exploitation, is still very much alive and kicking.

Again similarly, the African National Congress is not and never was a tolerant organization – except, of course, in its theoretical stance against certain intolerant practices of capital and minority white rule. I still remember how, during the exile years, everything possible was done in international forums to cut off the Pan-Africanist Congress's water and electricity.

Let's take another tack: South Africa's legacy of injustice and inequality can be tackled only by a combination of socialist solutions — and yet, all alternative socialist options had been squashed by the objective alliance of the NP government and the South African Communist Party. The Government simply put all leftists in the same 'red' bag of exile or prison; the Communists, intent upon retaining their ideological hegemony and thus more apprehensive of socialism or social democracy than of fascism, made sure that enriching schools of transformative thought were hounded into oblivion.

There is the paradox that, for the sake of building national unity, all alliances must be strengthened — and simultaneously certain relationships need clarification. What are you going to do about the superb coup of the SACP in managing to position so many of their stalwarts in the top power slots whilst having such an insignificant popular base? Or do you, like Mitterrand in the early eighties, intend to throttle them in a brotherly embrace?

We shall have to learn by rote the taboos and respect the non-negotiable principles of our new contract: never again racist discrimination, no more domination or corruption or exploitation (the workers must learn how to use the bosses intelligently), no cynical co-optation or hidden agendas. We have to acquire and nurture the right habits: tolerance, inventiveness, self-sufficiency, respecting the right of people to live out their cultures to the full. These must be enshrined as praxis. And you must keep a firm thumb on the merging security services who have as a common enemy the South African people.

We have to produce successes which can be measured morally. If we were to go down the Algerian road of a liberation movement bringing to power a largely exiled leadership which then sets about looting the state in a prolonged orgy of corruption (and some of your ministers already have this sweet tooth), we shall surely reap the same whirlwind: in due time a generation of fundamentalists will rise up to vomit the very ideals transported by national liberation — namely, tolerance and civilization and emancipation, and learning for all and the separation of powers, and national development.

Except that our version will be of the racist as opposed to the religiously fanatic variety.

Which is why, President Madiba, I suggest that one of your priorities ought to be a national convention on reconciliation which, to bring about the desired results, should be articulated region by region and district by district, and through all the professions and schools and lecture halls and media. This is not the prerogative or the playing field of politicians; it is a future base, emerging from the totality of civil society, for the definitive constitution which the newly elected parliament has been mandated to draft.

Let us not stop now. Already there is much to be proud of. Do you realize the impact of your example on Africa? *Jy het nie gekruip nie en jy het nie gevreet nie.* You have neither crawled nor tried to fatten yourself. Even more tongues have been set loose in Dakar and Nairobi by the objective lesson in democracy of a De Klerk relinquishing power and living to tell the story! How encouraging it will be to others if you were to keep up the standards of transparency, like publishing your earnings, for example. Africa can see now that power need not be abused and that there's the possibility of life beyond the loss of national office. There may even be room for effective opposition! Please continue being an apostate by showing us that it is not ineluctable for the winner to take (and devour) all.

I must tell you of a final private paradox even if it belies what I have written thus far. For the first time in more than thirty years I feel myself truly liberated from the perceived responsibility (and the self-binding temptation) to raise a political voice. Free, free at last not to endure my South Africanness as a burden or a shame or a job or even an example, free to be finally a footloose painter of metaphors and scribbler of colours!

Henceforth my contribution (and that of others of my ilk) will be: that our loyalty is a vigilant opposition; that any collaboration in the big project of constructing a South Africa in worthy accordance with the new realities born of dreams and of struggle will be predicated on principled criticism; that the assistance we can offer you, as father of the nation, is to treat you as a garden politician risking the mundane corruption of power inherent in all politics; that we shall oppose you through civil society; that we shall keep a particularly wary eye on the young whelps and the old party curs;

and that we shall grasp the freedom to be creative, each in her and his mother tongue, fully proud of our differences and of that which we share.

Yours faithfully.

Thinking Fire

Being neither philosopher nor historian, nor yet a naturalist, it is difficult for me to come to grips with the age-old dichotomy of nature and culture. As somebody who writes and paints though, I am dimly (sometimes grimly) aware that the tension evoked by the equation is central to creative reflection.

Man is the 'thinking reed', a conduit for consciousness, and the dilemma is already expressed by the formula. Does one shape oneself as reed by thinking? Or is thinking initiated and defined by the fact of being a reed? Could there be sky-thinking, rat-thinking, root-thinking — the way the reed thinks itself into separate being? When you shiver, are you sure it is not the wind which makes you move? In other words, is our awareness of consciousness dependent upon a backdrop of non-consciousness? But since we are of the ground, is not the expression of our singularity an alienation from our surroundings? Is thinking a loss of belonging? How do we merge again? Can the reed unthink itself?

It is argued that the universe, and therefore also our world, continually creates itself. This should be read together with the ancient Chinese concept that we are all involved in the ongoing recreation of a universe which exists, and has been completed, once and for all. If this is so, then our existence is the eternal rise and fall of life and death, sun and moon, Other and I, culture and nature — and our only possible quest that of harmony. This harmony, then, could have no moral connotation, since we are just breath coming and going.

But how can we *know* this? The words I write now come to me through the rustling of other 'reeds': what are the confines of our own inventions and expectations?

For some time I've been working on a series of poems called *Landberig* (Field Report). I remember at an early stage looking at the hills, 'proud as if I'd drawn them myself', and then laying down tasks: birds had to get names, the directions of winds had to be set out, trees given their lodgers and their complaints. These are attempts to insert myself into a given landscape or nature, to realize through a web of words an interaction. To say: 'Here I'll catch wind, and age in another country.' It may be inane along these lines to want to perceive what cannot be expressed, like the echoes we share with mountains. Words will remain words only.

The points I propose here should be seen as moments, with passing glances at schools and experiences I have barely a nodding acquaintance with. (They might as well be passing fancies expressing ignorance.)

What is culture? To some it is a manner of being — a set of expressions regulating our interaction with others, the community at large, our history, our identity, our destiny, our understanding. It could be seen as a code of values dictating norms and attitudes. Others may argue that it is only a structure, or again, that it is the necessary means by which we create ourselves subject to ethical and aesthetic convictions. What seems incontrovertible is that culture 'colours' our perception of reality, and from this perception our interests are usually defined: the interests of any given group are not abstract but derive from a shared 'experienced' awareness.

One could say, generalizing outrageously, that one of the differences between 'South' and 'North' is as follows: In Africa culture is a tissue of experiences, the uttering of cohesion, both a perception of social and natural environment and the environment itself (a tree can be a cultural artefact) — thus history, myth, tradition, relationships, taboos, magic, all to situate yourself within the immutable whole. In Europe, more torn apart, having moved through momentous accelerations, culture is a conscious tool in the continuing effort to establish identity and to 'master' natural forces. In the North the power quotient is built into culture; it is consciously applied to promote national cohesiveness, valorize history and justify superior values.

To generalize even more: to the Africans the world is a complex but unchanging environment into which you are born and where you adapt, posited on metamorphosis, because we are interchangeable with the land and vegetation and animals and spirits. To the European the world is a given that must be transformed.

> Too long the farm had gone to the dogs,
> bramblebushes took over wall and hedge.
> With old Neighbour's help I slash a clearing

around the pomegranate tree by the stable
whose roof has given way to emptiness:
                some yellow fruits
already cheek a riper red like stars grasping
all giddy and greedy for the light of another universe.

The tree had grown out of hand:
                we shape it,
and with the long blade
I whittle one of the thorny shoots
to fashion a shaft for the sickle
with which I intend to rout the weeds:
thus to arrange nature in a marginally ordered
field as grazing for starlight and the sickle-moon.

As 'thinking reeds' we are aware of our inevitable demise. As a species, like all others, we wish to survive. The world (our natural and social environment) is commonly experienced as hostile. Yet we are part of nature. Culture is also nature becoming conscious of itself.

The tragedy of the temporariness of conscious existence and of our lack of integration with nature leads to a sense of loss, of alienation even. Our first and original estrangement is from nature. We are caught in the dialectic of belonging and transformation which must lead to death.

There can be no creation without nature. We may be reworking the void but we cannot live as if we came from nowhere, not even as if we were unique. The efforts to overcome alienation can be either by transforming nature to suit our perceived needs, or by going back to the 'natural' or 'stream-of-consciousness'.

Our cultural relationship to nature is expressed in many forms. I'd like to identify a few. It may be a descriptive communion, often a symbolic projection, when we transfer to nature an expression of moods and sensations, and then we use the resulting picture to underline value judgements. Let's call this the romantic fashion.

It may be seen as attempts to harness nature, often leading to callous exploitation and ultimate destruction. An example which comes to mind is the shrinking Aral Sea, where rivers were displaced in order to reshape nature. (As someone recently remarked: 'The saddest job on earth must be that of a fisherman in the Aral Sea.') I don't need to multiply the examples – from burn-offs to atmospheric pollution to the soil's poisoning – only too well known. This is the utilitarian way.

It may be observed, admittedly on much smaller scale, where we rearrange nature according to aesthetic or spiritual sensibilities, sometimes linked to physical needs. I'm thinking, say, of the Japanese creation of mirrorscapes, of Arab gardens, of the European hortus. Here at least we see a sensitivity to the rhythms and internal shapes of nature, learning a million things from it, using it to awaken the soul. This is the meditative way.

But it is important to remember that there used to be other forms of awareness and knowledge: the Aboriginals whose world was sung, and it will die when the songs are forgotten; the pervasive and personalized presence of natural phenomena to the Bushmen, the Pygmies, the American Indians, the old Chinese hermits; even Catalan peasants, for instance, regulated their lives according to the natural forces, as still expressed in sayings and songs. These people were part of nature, they talked to it, took only what was needed, propitiated with sacrifices the anger provoked by an upsetting of harmony. This must have been the integrated way.

How do we see nature? Although the elements of our creativity spring from nature – rhythm, patterns, organic structures and cycles, the sounds of natural and animal worlds in our music – we are painfully aware of the limitations of our means, our words and our colours and our notes, when we try to apprehend or even copy nature. Culture defines and confines our understanding of nature.

Can we see Mont Sainte-Victoire without looking through the eyes of Cézanne, or Mount Fuji without having the vision of a Hokusai intervening? The chrysanthemum, the peach blossom – these became shorthand notes evoking set human emotions in Japanese and Chinese poetry. And how are we to extract the moon from Persian verse and make it fresh?

Perhaps we don't 'see' anything any more without the screen of culture. We discover through the known and can perceive at a given time only what the culture of that time permits us. Previous cultural embodiments become 'natural', we incorporate these in our field of reference, and our response to nature becomes conditioned by the cultural perceptions we are subject to. This must be why we find it normal to plunder, amend or rearrange nature in patterns of aesthetic norms or moral justifications.

It is interesting to see how these cultural visions change. We probably no longer relate to descriptions of nature of previous ages. Can we still 'understand' or 'read' the landscapes painted by Giotto or Ruysdael? It struck me forcefully when we visited the Australian Museum of Art in Canberra: for decades the European settlers saw and painted their new environment as square, gloomy and green English landscapes, and with time one can actually track the opening of the eye 'seeing new'. And yet, to their contemporaries, there must have been a fairly close fusion between 'outside' and 'inside'.

We measure our self-knowledge against nature: our sense of identity is defined by our depiction and enunciation. By these we trace its evolution.

Some people claim that the *constitution* of modernism flows from this share-out: the legitimacy of political power grows from society, that of scientific power from nature. In reality there's always been a 'bastardization' between nature and culture, giving rise to 'hybrid' objects, monsters and half-things — frozen embryos, numerical machines, data banks, robots which can register and translate emotions, hybrid crops, mind-altering drugs, whales with radio transmitters, gene synthesizers, plastic trees . . .

Culture doesn't make us more civilized. As our powers of manipulation increased we became more hostile and dangerous to nature, short-sightedly utilitarian, ultimately self-destructive. The spirit has become alert to the mixing of subjectivity and objectivity contained in a present which is the perpetual state of becoming. The result is that we produce more corpses than ever before, 'denatured' by the culture of communication.

The more refined we are, the more junk we distil. There are too many of us and we smother the world with our detritus. The survival instinct and the alienation from nature combine in materialist greed epitomized by the large-scale making of death machinery. Our 'priorities' are just faulty readings of the long-term interests of harmony. Or does the destruction of nature and the resulting promiscuity of mankind to fill the void induce a cultural death-wish?

This is our decadence: our means of transcription — our screens — have become reality to the extent that the 'undescribable', the nature we need to relate to, is now obliterated. Culture became nature. We forget that the finger pointing at the moon is not the moon.

Whereas this heightened a form of self-awareness and self-satisfaction (our descriptions constituting the real, making gods of us), it is also immoral. When we saw that there was no difference between signifier and signified, that we cannot get to the 'outside', we elevated the text to totality. We were afraid to succumb to the 'metaphysics of presence'.

Derrida says: 'There is nothing outside the text.' I say: 'The text, too, is an unravelling of the nothing. The text is a flimsy fig-leaf for inadequacy.'

Ah, how we love that which we destroy! Each generation lives with an image of nature embedded in its cultural expressions. This residual image programmes our destinies because it lays down the limits of the permissible. What is ours? Scorched earth? Butchered elephants and smoking forests and plastic seas and a decaying sky?

Is there a way back? An alternative? (I can say 'we must', or 'we ought to', knowing it is 'unnatural' to expect this to happen . . .) How sad that 'green awareness' or simple sanity should be referred to as 'alternative'!

Should we not return to simplicity, away from *hubris* to the intellectual poverty that will allow us to become enriched again by the totalness (or the void) of nature? For that we need to 'falsify the money' of human laws, as cosmopolitans and agnostics and cynics, the way Diogenes preached.

It probably means that people should be given a choice, that goodwill be mobilized, that the alienating factors be diminished (over-population, over-grazing, excessive standardization as in Europe, promiscuity, dehumanizing urbanization, the powerful running vast tracts of the earth to *their* advantage), that there should be teaching programmes, a devolution of power, above all *involvement.*

To unlearn power and forget mastery. To relearn patience and humility and respect and interaction and interdependence. To move away from homocentrism. We must relearn silence and the *expectant attitude*, so as to hear the presence. The essence of harmony is radical change.

Leiden, June 1992

Cold Turkey

*(Being shudders of withdrawal from the addiction of
believing that human nature could be ameliorated or human
behaviour changed for the better)*

To say 'The Writer and Politics' is to evoke a quandary. We hear
the din of distant battles and through ancient smoke we may still
read shifting lines of opposition and collaboration, treachery and
foolhardiness. There's a pungency on the air of burnt books and
scorched flesh, and sometimes we come across the remnants of ideas
and fermenting corpses like so many discarded arguments. Let us
provisionally see politics embodied as State, Party, Faith, or even
just the Correct Consciousness. Then we can trace throughout
history and in all cultures the story of the fatal attraction between
public power and writing. Too often the writers who became
ensnared in the incestuous relationship could survive only once they
gave up the struggle for justice to become politicians, or court
orderlies, or believers. Either way it would seem to have been, and
remain, a no-win position: the apostates were exiled from the areas
of shared experience, the social strategists ended up as political
cannon fodder.

   An ample crop of theories could be harvested from attempts to
circumscribe the interaction between writing and politics, or from
the description of how they use the same tool. A sharing detrimen-
tal to writing, I may add, which usually has but a lexicon of dead
words and a clutch of contaminated dreams to show for its involvement with politics.

   What are the shared premises and operation modes? Can it be the
manipulation of power? The creation of perceptions? Exploiting the
links and the breaks between reality and illusion? The sharpening or
the effacement (even the disfiguration) of the features of consciousness? To engender conscience? Moving cynicism from apathy to
active service? Do the two forms of public engagement really labour
the void in similar fashion? Doesn't writing also aim to be situated,

as politics projects itself to be, at the heart of life while holding out the hope of going beyond to an enhanced existence?

And can one reasonably hope to contribute any fresh insights to that which has already been observed to death? If I persist in seeing them as entities of an equation pulling and pushing over a changing field of mutual concerns, in what way did our times modify the meshing? I can only hope to step over the battlefield of stale abstractions by linking my remarks to a personal, quirky, and perhaps perverse trajectory; to explain how this pilgrim progressed from the never-never land of promise to the present location of nowhere.

For me, more and more, writing is about travelling and not about destinations. Identity is a passing creation, the sum of positions gained and evacuated during the trip. (I use 'gained' and 'evacuated' here as Gallicisms.) To be, it is normally assumed, one has to define in some form of mental defecation the social, political or cultural group you identify with. At the moment, if I'm not mistaken, I have no recognizable politics in the accepted sense. But this is not the same as being in a no-go zone.

Obviously — and at the risk of contradicting the distance or the abdication just penned out — I still adhere to a body of values. I remain partial and partisan. I insist upon making choices and acting accordingly, in speaking a mind as uncluttered as I can make it. I also try to be aware of the implications and the consequences of my ramblings.

The poet with a politics must come across as rather naïve, abrupt in her or his judgements, somewhat of a dreamer. After all, he or she is not a politician stricken by spasms of writing, but a writer first, offering (for example) the poem as the potential survivor of the act of death at the moment of writing. Thinking like this on one's hindlegs, furthermore, makes for a format of cut and dried statements encapsulating arbitrary reasoning.

Even so, and in order to advance, I'd itemize some of the values of left and right as follows. On the left one would expect to encounter the importance ascribed to the creative powers of imagination, and the concepts that every action has political significance; that economic forces should be politically accompanied for social pur-poses; that internationalism is a virtue and third-worldism a well-understood obligation; that deciphering the world is a complicated and open-ended but unavoidable process; that disagreeing with received truths is a necessary survival technique; that utopias must be envisaged just out of reach to keep us on our toes, but that realizing any such utopia will be an unmasking of death; that knowledge should be a transmission of the means to power to people, thus enabling them to take part in their own destinies; that nationalism and the prioritization of ethnicity are seizures of the collective mind bringing about generalized stupidity; that any configuration of society ought to be open and tolerant and responsive to spontaneity; that (to quote Blake) 'When the Reverence of Government is lost, it is better than when it is found.'

On the right then, there would be: aggressive or nostalgic nationalism, also called patriotism; the desirability of individual fulfilment as highest achievement; consensus politics; economics left to the experts; the coddling of minority rights and the extreme unction of affirmative action; virtual reality; politically correct thinking; eurocentrism; confusing power with right (as in, 'if I can afford to buy it I have the right to do so'); pragmatism (as in the integration of the attitude that there's not enough for everybody on this planet, so let us save the strong); charity; ethnic art; liberating the media from the dead weight of message or responsibility; the premise that there is no link between cause and effect except as in the case of investment and profit; beautiful bodies; safe sex as a placebo for existential nausea; ecology by way of maintaining the existing equilibrium between rich and poor; democracy as the avatar of capitalism.

I'm tempted to stretch even further the tenuous line of my thinking. To the left, revolution; to the right, politics. Because revolution negates the cynicism of 'the art of the possible' whereas politics is the arcane craft of disempowering the population. To the left, people as humans; to the right, 'the people' as masses, and élites. To the left, associations forming civil society; to the right, cabals, expert committees, vigilantes, brotherhoods, the Vanguard Party, the State with its nomenklatura. To the left, understanding or confusion; to the right, 'correct' understanding or indifference. To the left, the Way; to the right, the Truth. To the right, banks and the IMF, Muslim fundamentalists, Switzerland, the security establishment and all manner of political police and informers and pimps, arms dealers, radical chic, cultural workers, the USA, the New World Order, freedom fighter leaders, caviar socialists, postmodernism, Billy Graham, the North, the Pope, Czar Leonid Yeltsin the First. To the right also the invidious choice presented as: vote for me, my party may be bad but that of our opponents is even more horrible. To the right, similarly, the Stalinist premise that one must keep (to) the ranks of discipline when faced by a common enemy. (In South Africa, incidentally, this imprecation translates as 'One settler one bullet', or 'No education before liberation'.) To the left, the fumbling search for more justice; to the right, intervention by the power players in the name of human rights.

The politics you practise is one way of impacting upon the world in which you live; it is also part of the spectrum through which that world impinges on your awareness. This dialectic brings to mind a story I was told years ago by Beauford Delaney, an American painter who lived in Paris. Beauford's great-grandmother had been born before the disappearance of slavery. An old gentleman she knew, let's call him Freedom for argument's sake, used to be the property of a one-legged slave-holder. Whenever the owner bought new shoes he would pass one, the left one for which he had no need, to Freedom. Freedom would wait until he had two 'new' left shoes before donning them as a pair. By the end of his life, Freedom, who'd started off with two perfectly normal feet, hobbled along on a crippled right clubfoot. When Beauford told this tale his body would shake and tears would roll down his cheeks.

We live in extraordinary times, confronted by a rapidly shifting series of momentous events, buffeted by false hopes, but also brought face to face with unpalatable disillusions. The horrors we witness, and which we seemingly can do nothing about, have broken the back of our capacity for outrage. As lounge animals we sit there, flooded by instant global information and the immediate deceptions of trivialization. We are neither called upon to invest an effort at understanding nor to participate in the digestion of communication, and we have our impotence shoved down our throats. The need for survival oblivion has reduced our languages to advertisement jingles for bland politics, smoothing the texture of our means of perception. We transferred our memories to data bases and are losing the transformative art of remembering. Even our inventiveness is now being defined by the parameters of soundbites and the contours of computer programs. Our imaginations are ever more skylined by the hysterical and narcissistic cry for live-time novelty. We have all sorts of festering answers to questions that can no longer be asked. We don't even get drunk any more. Is that which we perceive reality or lie? Suddenly there is nowhere to look forward to and nothing to be nostalgic about.

One of the fond conceits I grew up with was that writers were intelligent people. (One of the biggest mistakes the belief that writing ought to be a game of intelligence.) And, because they were so often the critics of an existing order, I furthermore took the politically conscious writers to be fired with a refined sense of ethical awareness. Now I know it is more complicated. Writers, blinded perhaps by the assumed influence of their insights and flattered by the shadow of power, are often the last to read the times, to recognize the failure of their pompous dreams, to decode the manipulation of words and the juggling of ideas in the fruit machines of perceptions. We do not want to see how crippled we are by the fact of being parlour guests in the mansions of the rich. We cajole and vie for acceptance. We all want to be liked and stroked for making sense.

Seldom are writers summoned to shoulder responsibility for the false routes they enticed so many people to embark upon. In Europe, for instance, a generation of 'thinkers' who fob themselves off as writers, sad television donkeys really, have 'progressed' from the pious left of pie in the sky to the abrasive right of money in the pocket without, apparently, sacrificing any credibility or self-assurance. So that where we once had these public consciences writing and marching against imperialist wars in Vietnam or colonialist repression, or simply concerned about the hounding of 'illegal' immigrants at home to the third and fourth generation, we now find the aberration of those same leading lights raucously clamouring for Libya to be invaded or Serbia to be bombed. The play may have changed; the important thing is to be on stage!

Take the Gulf War. It would be interesting to analyse how a man like President Bush – certainly nobody's paragon of moral probity or intellectual finesse – managed to bamboozle a gaggle of European intellectuals into baying for Arab blood.

The general attitude seems to be: let us construct a tight Europe, let us build a wall around our accumulated privileges and keep out the hungry and the dirty and the poor. We're all right, Jack; it is an idealist delusion to be concerned about those to the south and the east of us. And this at a time when roads in Europe are again clogged with refugees, when the notion of 'ethnic purification' has once more reared its hoary head, while Africans trying to sneak into the paradise of paler skins are drowning in the Gibraltar Straits.

No wonder that so many writers have withdrawn to the campuses, there like alienated baboons to deconstruct, to eviscerate and sniff at the innards of our art – the phonemes and the signifiers.

Or let us consider Africa. A few months ago I finished an African journal. In the process of writing I came across some old documents – including the 'Large Illustrated Description of Africa' by Olfert Dapper, published in Amsterdam in 1668. In it are to be found the most outlandish descriptions of exotic animals, like the unicorn, or another with the body of a wolf and a man's legs, and of tribes who walk on their heads with the feet in the air, as also others with their mouths and eyes in their bellies. The thought struck me that to the world at large Africa has always been a dark hinterland of the psyche, perforce unexplored, a sunken continent of the unknown or the subconscious upon which to project all the delicious phantasies of magic and death. An updated variation of this fabulation is, to the outside world, the depiction of present-day Africa as a continent where dying is a mass pastime, best left alone to its starvation, desertification, tribal wars, AIDS, and the implosion of its social structures.

In the South generally (under this generic term I refer to the so-called 'peripheral' world when compared to the rich northern countries, to those areas of our planet where the majority of mankind live and die, also known as the developing or emergent or Third World) – in the South, then, the activities of writing and politics often are more complementary than they would appear to be in the North. One reason for this must be that the struggle for dignity against an unfair power balance is closely intertwined with cultural resistance. Politics there still crackle with basic existential needs, including the striving to revalorize or shape a cultural identity that has been humiliated. This, incidentally, is the easy part, if painful: to resist, to point a finger at history and at the hyenas across the border, to fight vested injustices. The difficulties come when we have to imagine viable alternatives, when we realize that the ends do not justify the means, when we see that the troubles are caused by our weaknesses rather than by the strength of the hereditary exploiters. The unease also comes when we observe that our noble writers fattened on protest are as adept as their Northern counterparts at becoming scheming and demagogic politicians.

I do not intend to denigrate the importance of African writers bringing to the attention of a wider audience the history and aspirations and complex cultures of our continent. But I have sat in on too many gatherings where all the old litanies of being victims were trundled out, laced with the posturing of pseudo-revolutionaries bearding Northern sensitivities. I too wallowed in the trough of self-pity. Often I think that the weaker we are the more eloquent our protest becomes. Mostly though, these are stratagems for blackmailing the North's bleeding heart for con-science money. So often, for example, do we bewail the fact of being dispossessed of our native tongues. And yet I know of very few African writers willing to get stuck into the task of establishing networks of publishing, distribution and education in indigenous languages. I don't see us creating the facts on the ground, counting on our own abilities and sharing these with the disinherited popula-tions who find themselves arbitrarily subjected to the rip-off struc-tures called 'independent states' from which only the élite few or the military many benefit. The sad fact is that African writers by choice or out of necessity or alienation write for non-African readers.

And so on to South Africa. I intimated at the outset of my paper that I find myself nowhere now. It is true that I have been back to that no man's land, but I soon found that I couldn't fit in, that I could neither condone the conversions of those who switched overnight from being privileged members of the master class to pen-carriers for the liberators (without missing a goosestep, as it were), nor continue unquestioningly to support in the name of 'unity' the cause I helped struggle for. 'Unity in the face of the enemy', I found, was the strategy exerted to establish a new hegemony of mediocrity where the notion of quality, for example, was decried as 'bourgeois irrelevant'. The fragrance of revolution had been blown away by the stench of politics.

Only natural, you may want to say: the naïve dreaming had to be put to rest. But I had hoped that we could grasp and carry forward the vision of our uniqueness posited on the incredibly rich diversity of origins and modes of expression, that we could deci-sively rally around our purity, which is a profound *métissage* of cultures, and that this would enable us to reach out to the worlds of Africa and Europe and the East even. National reconciliation could be effected, I thought, on condition that there's no white-out of memory, provided, I said, that we break open the silences, that we get all the repressed *non-dits* out in the open.

It was not to be. Why not? To my mind there are many reasons. By the time the liberation movements were allowed again to operate legally inside the country and the exiles permitted to return, two essential dimensions of our dreamspace had caved in – 'virtual socialism' had collapsed, 'national liberation' on the African model, so it turned out, had led to disastrous misery nearly everywhere. (It must be said that the West did next to nothing to help the poor suckers build a viable and defendable alternative dispensation. Could it be because consumerism is the only Western ideology offered for sale, with arms and munitions and the attendant high-tech toys as surplus currency with which to open the markets, and thus that the only example proposed would be democratic death on the hire-purchase system?)

We had become flabby and arrogant in exile, spoilt like harem women on the sweetmeats of international support. Wasn't our cause the moral basket case of the world? Exiles talking about the plight of their situation and of the suffering back home, you must know, are like fish learning to breathe on dry land – there will be much gasping and heaving, but ultimately we are only that: fish on dry land. Now the international community suddenly lost interest. They found other fish to fry. Ethnicity came back into fashion, the break-up of states became plausible, Africa was written off and we were now part of Africa.

For too long had we lied to others and ourselves – and most criminally to those struggling and waiting inside – in the name of mobilization, about the extent of the 'armed struggle', about how well we had thought through and prepared for the future, about the nature of our alliances and the excellence of our internal democracy. For too long, in fact, did we put off the need for democratization. And we had learnt too much from the enemy, hoping to steal its power by imitation, adopting its ruthless and autocratic and secretive ways. We made the townships ungovernable, and now they are and remain indeed ungovernable.

And in the initial euphoria we misread the situation. The State had never given up on their war against the population. War continued in the name of peace; it is spreading its poison and destruction still. We underestimated the commitment of State securo-crats to leave a scorched earth to the future. Worst of all, human life had been made too cheap. Now, with the incumbent Government fanning the fires, pitching group against group, dislocating the black community, the slaughtering has attained its own momentum. Who can ever again rule without repression?

The ongoing filthy war in South Africa is to my mind not so much about a centralized and unified majority-ruled state as opposed to a federal dispensation with decentralized power – no, it is (or ought to be) about the devolution of power and the sharing of responsibilities. It is about the contours and conflicts and cutting edges and tangent planes between State and civil society. When there's a conflation (willed by politicians) of State and Party, State and workers, State and culture, State and ideology – then you have a dictatorship, be it of the Party (supposedly on behalf of the urban and rural proletariat), or the military or an élite or an individual. Under those circumstances the citizen becomes what György Konrad called a *Staatsmensch*, somebody who has integrated the notion of himself as pawned possession and expression of the State.

In South Africa the State belongs to the Broederbond (a fraternal semi-secret society of the male white Afrikaner élite), laying claim to it in the name of the history and the interests of a narrowly defined ethnic and cultural group, the Afrikaners, and farmed out to thick-headed administrators, cruel and cowardly securocrats, rapacious captains of our capitalism of the primitive colonial kind. Of course the Afrikaner state is built on sand – we're neither racially 'pure' nor culturally homogeneous or exclusive – and all the spilled blood did not consolidate the foundations. At present the ANC élite – directed by its own Broederbond, the South African Communist Party – are being co-opted by or otherwise infiltrating the State. The Party is investing the terrains of trade unionism, culture and higher education, to gather the captives for the unaltered State which will in future be denoted as 'democratic', 'united' and 'of the people'. So far the ANC has been allowed to sidestep the contradictions between nationalism and democracy in a multi-national state simply because the democratically correct objective of 'majority rule' brings with it the unspoken inevitability of black rule. In the meantime racism continues unabated, no longer needing laws to bolster the structures and practices of iniquity. Social and economic dissolution may have reached the point of no return.

If I insist upon this conundrum (to be found in different declen-

sions all over Africa) it is because I believe we can save ourselves only by strengthening the democratic capacities of civil
society (the trade unions, cultural groupings, the media, citizens'
associations . . .); by vigorously confining politicians to their rule as
servants of the community, counteracting their 'natural' tendency
to feed off society's labour, to instantly pollute and corrupt us
with their arrogant power (some riches are after all still *produced* and
not just stolen from the beggar's hat of speculation); and especially
by recognizing the State for what it is – our necessary cancerous cyst
which must be kept within bounds by a judicious mixture of combat
and care.

I believe that such a 'permanent revolution', this harmony of
dynamic change (where the deontologies and responsibilities of the
various groupings will be constantly assessed and buttressed, by
hook or by crook), is not a 'luxury' as thinking Africans sometimes
aver, but a staple necessity for public hygiene. I should also say that
my conception of the State (and therefore of power to the people)
does not flow from a liberal tradition, but grows from some half-
forgotten yearnings of the left. In this vision, I think, the State
(ultimately the homeland of politicians) will be a defined and
picketed organism, as democratically controlled and accountable as
possible, guaranteeing the separation of powers, mediating conflict-
ing interests, using its accumulated assets as repository of the
common good to provide protection for the weak and to promote
social justice for all. *Nada más!*

We all saw the light at the end of the tunnel before the roof
caved in. Or, as a sad poet put it: the shit has hit the fan, but it
doesn't matter – the fans don't work any more.

Did History finally devour Imagination? Is it true then that
nothing can ever grow again on the killing fields? What about the
writers? I found, by and large, two categories: those who know but
do not speak up, tongue-tied by guilt or a false sense of solidarity;
the others who believe that repeating the mumbo-jumbo of slogans
constitutes revolutionary literature. And then there are those, the
commissars who never wrote, or only incidentally, who now run
the 'structures' of 'cultural workers'. Too many writers believe they
have their noses pointing towards fragrant promises of the republic
of peace just over the hill when they are in fact locked in on
slipstreams from the comfortable and perfumed buttocks of politicians digging for power to the Party.

When I pointed this out — and I could have been wrong, as so often before; how much I still hope to be proven wrong! — comrades asked: 'Why can't you be happy now we've won?' Former friends accused me of being a bird of doom (and perhaps of ill omen), coming periodically to shit all over the beloved country before returning to my comfortable perch abroad. Newspaper editors admonished me to stop whining so as not to scare the children and to just go away to the luxury of so-called exile. Anonymous readers, freed at last to show what they had thought all along of this smug moral magistrate, wrote to say: 'Fuck you! Fuck you good!'

So where does that leave me? Where do I stand? What is my politics? It may shock you when I say I find this personal *tabula rasa*, this zero degree of functionality, rather exhilarating.

This is what I have learnt: It is better to be writing and painting than to be mind-sucked by television's gospel of stupidity. Nobody ever said that suffering leads to wisdom or tolerance, but not being able to express terror leads to new permutations of terror. Writing may be a lie, but it is a small one compared to the big lie of politics. Even ivory towers need central heating. Put a human in a position of power and he or she will abuse it instantly, or soon after. Commitment of the artist to the evolution of ethics is not a choice, it is a breathing, a rhythm, because it partakes of creation. Writing will be political because it incarnates a ceaseless struggle with the resistant and approximate matter of perceptual awareness, and because this struggle will mouth in shared codes and is thus social. Writing, which is writing the self and rewriting the world, is best at home in civic society. There is a dialectical relationship between 'repeating the known' as a way of flexing the sense of belonging, and inventing the private road of individuality with madness at the end.

Politics is a power trip, but no longer the dominant factor among the other powers, such as (not exhaustively): the Mafia, the media, the empires of drugs, the arms dealers, the banks, the multinationals, academies, administrations, armies, the security establishments ... Language is the memory of power, and memory the power of pain. The State is a blind mirror which will steal your face. Writing which aims at transforming awareness can be about searching (for) the margins to stretch the limits; politics however moves down the centre from compromise to collusion to corruption.

At last we know that not all problems need to have solutions, because some solutions can be more disastrous than the problems. Politics may be as much of a fiction as writing is. Everywhere we look we see the implosion of public morals. Socialists are even more greedy for protocol and patronage than conservatives are. Every North needs a South (it may even fabricate an internal one as we see happening in Europe now), if only to provide for the movement of disequilibrium.

The nature of man is bestial, the concept of progress futile and redundant, but struggle for decency continues. There will always be history because there will always be dreaming, and therefore conflict. No gain is permanent and permanence is not a gain either. It is the walking that life is all about; the goal is only a certain dimension or configuration of absence which will help to elicit activity. Knowing meaning is a good way for preparing the unknowing. To tell a story is to activate a dream.

I must keep running after myself so as not to lose sight of the dark light of creativeness: that is, subverting the hegemony, unhinging the unstoppable process of accretion and accumulation, rattling the skeleton and the empty bowl of the mind, taunting that powdered death called Respectability, keeping the cracks whistling, fighting for revolution against politics. Aesthetics and ethics cannot be separated.

It is important to take responsibility for the story. Imagination is politics. He who travels alone travels fastest, but in the company of friends you go further . . .

Saint Louis, Missouri, 21 October 1992

The Lines Have Fallen unto Me
in Beautiful Places

(how to help a character out of a story)

A strange thing happened on the way through my last published book, *Return to Paradise*. Those who read it will remember that it was the account of a pilgrimage to where the navel-string lies buried – a memory of the heart, but also a region of the imagination. My wife, Lady One, accompanied me all the way. Throughout our journey we were dogged by a rather obnoxious character. From the outset of the story he would surface at odd moments to taunt me with sarcastic remarks. It was as if he considered it his duty to rub my nose in the faulty observations and the flaky conclusions I was committing to paper. He would present himself as Mr Lexie or Mr Eilex or Mr Ixele, and on one or two occasions simply as Mr X, as if he didn't know who he really was, or was reluctant, perhaps, to decline his true identity.

His presence was a mute accusation. Once or twice Lady One asked who the man was, and what did he want. Then I pursed my mouth and talked him away. When it came to editing the bulky manuscript, however, it was suggested that I should leave out altogether this shadowy figure blocking the background like an unresolved nightmare, this dog barking without a voice. It was felt that such a spectre from the past would detract from the veracity and the limpidity and the *present tense* of the story. Moreover, he had no political significance. Thus he became invisible, like a deleted word or thawed ice.

I complied because it is advisable to streamline attention, but I've been ill at ease ever since. Somehow I was still tied to him by guilt. For me the book was closed, and the past, after having been revisited, buried – yet this character was left hanging in my reminiscences, twirling in the sough of words while dispensing the insidious odour of putrefaction. He had to be cut down. This is why I must backtrack, as it were, to where the bone was buried, to help him out of his misery. Those of you who were with us on the earlier trip will remember a myth that used to be alive for the Bushmen, those ancient inhabitants of Gondwanaland who have long since been integrated with the dust: for them the rainbull lived in the underground source; when in a trance the shamans would enter the earth (walking upside down!) to go and beseech the rainbull for water and abundant hunting.

At a certain stage we found him, dressed in a dirty white suit and red shoes, along the road leaving Middelburg. I stopped the car — nagged by this sense of responsibility — to offer him a lift. From a hawker he'd bought a miniature windmill made of tin, an emblem of the Karoo. No wind to turn the sunflower-faced head, but then too there was no water to be had. This he clutched to his chest. He said his name was Elixe ('close to the water of youth') and that he was going our way. The route took us into the sombre arguments of massive mountains overlooking, as we reached the top of the pass, grey and purplish plains. In ancient times Bushmen would have lived in caves up here and study the distance for the dust of migrating antelopes. On the front seat next to me Lady One had fallen asleep; in the rearview mirror I caught Elixe's eye, he smirked and winked. Our conversation sounded like the continuation of previously interrupted thoughts. (This *complicity* bothered me.)

He: How's your unwieldy book coming along? Are you still running after structure? You always confused allusions with meaning and pattern-making with structure when, in fact, it was nothing more than decorative weaving.

So he was aware that I was experiencing our peregrination through the country like the writing of a book! It was irritating that he should know me so well. I thought of making the point that the only visible sign of the rainbull's presence would have been the weaver birds plaiting nests in the wind of trees growing near some subterranean stream. But it was better to laugh it off.

I: That's democracy for you. The surface is important. We live in a nonsense world and the only way forward is to create tension by embellishing the form in point and counterpoint, repetition and break, reference and counterfeit. To give the shimmering illusion of meaning. What other purpose does illusion serve? Like the windmill which is a creaking prayer wheel to suck water from nowhere.

He: Ah, so you're implying that the illusion of meaning is exactly the meaning of illusion. Even the devil will not recognize his own in such a maze of mirrors. Tell me now — this is changing the subject — why do white people in Gondwanaland insist so much on being accepted as Africans? Why must they make a confession of faith as if perpetually on the verge of wishful thinking? Or sinking. Don't they know who they are? Is it because no one in the world will own up to them? Are they like ice that cannot thaw?

I ventured the idea that the continuous crystallization of identity had always been a local obsession, the white settlers were after all the prolongation of a primitive utopian striving. And then they were orphaned. The sea was burning and they'd lost the art of reading wind and waves. Their hands rotted; since they had an imagined past they were obliged to create themselves. Their frontier became a heaven and the continent consumed them.

He: And they can never write the landscapes out of their system. The natives hereabouts are not bothered by any sort of dichotomy between environment and man. *Their* trees and mountains speak with the voices of forebears. As for us [he leaned forward in a familiar fashion], can we say the lines have fallen unto us in beautiful places? Our initiation was a life-sickness. We had to go on writing ourselves out there to fit a tongue to the mouth. And then we lost the language. Are the lines not also nooses?

His breath was cold and malicious in my neck.

A few weeks later Lady One and I were in Pietersburg, a biggish agglomeration in the Northern Transvaal. We were taken to the university spread among huge boulders quite some way out of town, where I was to kick the word around with a few lecturers and students. Among them there was even a philosopher with beard and a smile lacking several teeth, a Robben Island graduate — that is, an ex-political prisoner. At the far end of the table I noticed the familiar face of Mr X. He gave me a long dry look. The discussion was desultory. Suddenly he interrupted with one fist on the table:

He: You know, your quandary is the typical unease of the returnee coming face to face with a dead dream.

I: Dead dream? No, I think what we have to deal with here are two kinds of writers – the violin pissers and the comrades. Or, rather, those who relieve themselves with aesthetic fingers, and the others, who do it with clenched fists. We need both. As long as they only do it in their violins and don't abuse their neighbours' ears or salad beds or tombs. But it is true that the local writers walk around with soaked instruments.

He: Come now, don't let the dead dream poison you – let's suppose I'm the typical indigenous writer who stayed put, and you are the returning exile. What do you say?

(I said to myself: *He of all people? How sick can one get!*)

I: I'd suggest we exiles are entitled to our pound of flesh, we stayed pure, out there we had to sacrifice much. But we gained a broader vision of the world and its ways. We became well-seasoned internationalists.

He: Oh really? While you people sat on fat behinds at the tables of the World Council of Churches, the High Commission for Refugees, the United Nations, while you hobnobbed with the power dealers of international solidarity, we had to harness ourselves to the struggle with our tails caught in the traps of survival. This is where we danced. We were guarding the flame of resistance. Now you want to come and make pigs of yourselves with the fattened calf!

I: Listen, if you wanted to dirty yourselves with politics, that was your choice. Writing is writing and politics is bullshit. Unlike you cultural workers, we had to struggle with the fragile utterances of a confused creativity.

He: Were we not also writers and painters and film-makers? But somebody had to do the dirty work. We gave of ourselves on behalf of the future. All those poems we never got around to writing, the images gathering dust. We too have dead children to mourn. Comrade, you know we stuck it out against bourgeois élitists, university aesthetes and other liberal bleeders. And now we have a truly democratic non-racist popular culture, free from your white Western hierarchy, from sexism and so-called quality! You individualists who lived off our suffering, you've had your day. We have closed our minds; we are now entering the circle of arguments. The time for arse-licking is finished.

I: A writer is a writer is a writer. One judges an axe by its ability to chop and you can't make a screwdriver out of a carrot. Struggle literature, resistance literature, these were good and necessary. Now we ought to play out the literature of shifting the lines which have fallen unto us in beautiful places lest they become ropes around our necks. To hell with new hegemonism in the name of the most popular common denominator!

He threw back his head and laughed, as the saying goes, like a whore taking a child for christening. He laughed like a windmill in full flight of rusty blades. He laughed like a rusty blade slitting a throat. He laughed like a whoreson dunked in cold baptismal water.

We are on the eve of leaving the country for Europe. The telephone rings. This time it is for me. Mr X on the line, I listen for a long time but will not report this conversation. No traces must remain. Things must come to a head. Lady One and her friend Rehena went off to shop. I leave a note saying I've been urgently summoned to Cape Town, Nelson Mandela wants to see me, I'll be back tomorrow. I manage to get on a late flight for Mother City.

Night thoughts. D. F. Malan Airport. Sneaking back like a thief. According to my nephew Hétéros the family coat-of-arms indicates that our ancestors were wolf hunters. Must be why we are dogs. Hire a car. Turn up collar against the wind. Don't look at mountain. Sweet smell of late summer. Drive out to Paradise House.

There are small shards of paradise left in this shattered world – this house is one, so is Gorée Island, and Timbuctu with its mouth full of sand, there's a *finca* in Spain called Can Ocells and the village of Poble Nou in the Ebro delta with palm trees set humming by mosquitoes, there's an oasis in some russet mountains with a walled-in garden called Wildedruif, there's a town on the brown Mekong, there's a tower in Paris from where you can observe the hurried clouds . . .

The house is dark. He heard me coming even though I parked a distance away and walked up the steep rise of loose shoal. He's standing on the front stoep overlooking the immensity of a light-devouring sea. A front window is shattered and a toy windmill is lying on the cement. 'Don't worry, it's all I took. Mine anyway. I needed it to see if the wind is blowing right. Don't want to get tangled in the branches.'

I brought with me some photos I'd like to show. He strikes match after match and we comment on the images of people we shared on this visit which now draws to a close. (A reader of *Return to Paradise* will recognize them.) By the brief flare of light, which poets would compare to a lifetime, I notice that the obscure hump on his back is a pair of wings smelling of decomposing meat – he mounted these wings by sewing and sticking and singeing together all the wings of the birds he ever killed.

'There's nothing like collective memory,' he says. 'Look, here I am with Colonel Wadd,' I say. 'And here are all the Foxes and Angelo Mosca and Bogar and Zena and the Slabberts,' he remarks, 'that's me in the dark glasses and the shorts, you have a big belly.' 'This is me with the Venda poets,' I say. 'Ah yes,' he agrees. 'Look at how I'm lifting my beard to tickle Unum's nostrils. And look at me here at the French party, a real red-chested bird.' He's running out of matches. 'She's a good photographer, our Lady One,' he observes. 'Yes,' I agree, 'but photos warp reality.'

It is dark. 'We don't have to lie to one another,' he says. 'That's about the only thing we don't have to do,' I concur. 'Anyway, you have no images of Unum or Peinêtre or Dog,' he murmurs. 'It will be difficult to put Dog together again, his hand has rotted, Unum alone knows where it is buried. Unum's nostrils must be twitching,' I say laughing. 'And Comtesse Delafesse was always looking for a snake in her bed.'

'The moon will rise soon, we must go,' he says. 'Do you have the rope?' I ask. He is apologetic: 'I took Mrs Fox's washing-line up the hill there, I hope she won't mind.'

'What must I do with the windpump . . . afterwards?' I ask. 'It is yours now,' he answers with a barked laugh. 'May it bring you water. It will start chattering when you approach the rainbull's subterranean labyrinth. Come. You must be brave.' We start moving in the direction of the big black bluegum. 'Here, take the matches.'

'There is this to remember, son of my elder brother: nothing happens that has not happened before. Our brother has gone from us. A man dies even if he be praised, he disappears even if he be loved, and sinks out of sight even when we weep for him. It is not for a man to lick his wounds – only a dog does so. Yes, "a fine eating-mat soon wears out with use". My father's son has gone, handsome man that he was. Be ye comforted; strengthen yourself, and move about among people . . .'

As we start climbing up the tree (he's having difficulty with the clumsy wings) he says: 'Now repeat with me.' We recite together: *'lento umntu iyemka noko ibonwayo.'* ('The most renowned man must die.')

We are in the tree. I'm perched slightly higher than he is. 'Do what you must do,' he admonishes. He's tied the rope around his neck. I take the other end and attach it to the sturdy branch upon which I'm sitting. 'Just let me get my breath,' he says. 'It's a beautiful sight from up here . . . The lines have indeed been gracious to me.'

'Yes,' I observe, 'but it's dark.' He asks: 'And so, has the break been consumed?' I: 'The break's been there for thirty odd years. That's where *you* came in, remember?' He: 'And you couldn't heal it.' I: 'At what price? When you break, when you start speaking the silences, you also sacrifice being part of the natural dimension of social environment, you tear the tissue with your bitter words.' He: 'But you are free to go to the end of your untethered mind.' I: 'Yes, although the mind is a passing phase, and the end of the road is to be nowhere.' He, gently: 'So you returned and tried to bridge the gap with reams of silences.' I: 'But I'm too far gone, ridiculously old, nobody could give a damn!' He: 'Oh, they do, you poor fellow, they do. They whisper behind your back. Can't you hear the small knives? They point fingers like sharpened blades and say — has he always been a fool or did he only recently become one?' I laugh: 'The more fool you!' He says: 'Okay, this is it. Here I come!'

While holding on with one arm to my branch I jump down on his, shouting: *'Phakathi!'* (which means, 'Get inside!' 'Kill!'); it snaps under our combined weight, he slips off, the rope pulls taut with the twanging sound of a plucked string, he crashes free. I hoist myself up on my branch, sit a while to catch my breath, climb down. Goodbye, Mr Exile, goodbye. The dark shape twists, twists, thrashes, kicks, jerks, shudders, twists, relaxes, starts swinging slowly (like a lullaby). The tree is strangely quiet, strange and bitter fruit, the wind must have turned. I chant softly:

> 'This is the bird whose flesh I have never tasted
> With the councillors who were eating it;
> Bird with the blood-spot on your throat,
> Better luck-bringer than other birds.'

I wait. It looks as if the form is flying even though there's no breeze. I sing again:

> '*Tshoko ji!* I'm a hangman!
> Fear not, little chap!
> I'm the courageous bird,
> Well-versed in warfare!
> Even the pied crow is under my sway,
> For I am the bravest of birds;
> With my bill I stick my prey by its head on the thorns,
> Hanging it on a tree.'*

I wait. The moon has risen. I climb back up past the swaying figure. I touch it in passing. It is as soft and feathery as my own imagination. I untie the washing-line, the figure drops straight down with a snapping of twigs and a tearing of leaves. I'm getting tired. The wings have been ruined, feathers are scattered all over. I drag the body back to the stoep. I rest. I try to prise open the broken window and slash my hand on the jagged pane. Curses! The blood wells up black in the moonlight.

I climb through the window with the toy windmill and put it back near the fireplace where we, Lady One and I, left it nearly a week ago when we departed from Mother City. Mr Exile had forgotten it in our car on the road near Middelburg and we didn't know how to return it to him. Mrs Fox kindly allowed us to abandon it in Paradise House. How will he find it now? There are traces of Lady One's scent in the rooms. I rest. The hand is throbbing but the bleeding seems to have stopped.

Climb out the window again. Lift the body across my shoulders, with these wings I shall never fly, rest, start stumbling down the slope towards the car as if carrying a sick ancestor. Fit him into the boot. I have to fold his legs, he's lying jackknifed in the foetus position, the moonlight reflects off his bared grin.

I drive halfway up Red Hill. Rest. The hand aches. Drag him off the road into a clearing in the undergrowth. The legs remain bent. Can *rigor mortis* set in this rapidly? I gather leaves, twigs, dry branches. Curse. I rest. Pile the wood around him and set it alight with the matches he gave me. The whitish suit takes fire, the grin is maddening, the smoke gets thicker and has the sickly smell of

---

* These chants can be found in *Xhosa Oral Poetry*, by Jeff Opland.

scorched meat. Wind has come up again. (The Cape is known for its capricious climate.) A few sparks blew on the grass which is now smouldering. I curse and start stomping out the fire. What the hell do you think you're doing? Want to burn down the mountain? Have you no sense of responsibility toward the community? Tear off some green branches (hurting my hand even more) and start beating out the fire. Roll the rigid half-singed corpse off the pyre and kick sand over the embers. Pull him back to the car.

It won't be night much longer. I prop him up on the seat next to me. We rest. Hurry now. I drive down the coast road, turn right at Muizenberg — it is too early for joggers — and continue to Strandfontein. I point out the sights to him. This will be the quietest spot. Given that there will be no anglers! Please, God (hallowed is the Name), give the fish a chance!

Ah, this long strip of beach stretching from Muizenberg to Gordon's Bay used to be part of the Absurd Theatre of Apartheid. They divided it into strips for every population group, those fascists with the pig-thoughts and the hairy lips. The sector set aside for blacks was called *Sonwabe* ('Happiness'!); there was a slice for browns, a sliver for Indians, and they even thought of developing an enclosure for Chinese. That fell through when research showed that there were only fifty Chinese families living in the Peninsula, and they weren't enthusiastic beachcombers either. Maybe they felt no affinity with those vanished Khoi known as *Strandlopers* (literally, 'beach walkers') who died out because of their excessive diet of shellfish. The beach looks deceptively safe, the sea tame. Many people drowned here over the years, sucked in by hungry waves. Food for watery thought. No beacons now. New South Africa. No people in sight.

I stop the car. Shuffle down to a deserted stretch of sand silvered by a dying moon. Start scooping a grave in the wet sand. What shall I say to my poor hand — sliced, half-burnt, bruised by branches, tired of writing, now caked with sand? It is getting lighter, a heavy grey dawn. The sea sings with closed mouth deep in its throat. Maybe night must be digested to make room for day. Must have a pee soon or bladder will burst. Do whales still venture this far? Remember reading how they spend time in False Bay with new-born calves. The old days. Can't waste time on existential questions now. The future is a sequence of present events. Always. Walk on!

Shift the blackened corpse down to the grave. Nobody will know what 'race' he was. Try to make him lie down. The legs won't straighten. Put him in a sitting position. The hole is not deep enough. Bad luck. Too tired to start all over. I have only one good hand. What stupidity! Cars will be coming by soon. Hurry!

Scoop sand around the sitting figure. His shoulders and head stick out. He's facing the sea, the incoming waves. He'll be thirsty. Never mind.

Back up the road. I drive to the airport, hand back the hired car, the jaunty black attendant says: 'Been *jolling* [partying] the whole night, hey?' 'The Cape is a *lekker* [enjoyable] place,' I say. Into the washroom to tidy up. Damn this hand. I only hope there aren't any acquaintances on the plane.

Back in Johannesburg I phone Chisi (the chauffeur working for the friends where we're staying) to come and fetch me. He says another of their cars has been stolen recently. 'It is all Mandela's fault.'

At home Lady One is spitting with fury. 'Where have you been? What are you going to invent this time? And what happened to your hand? *Siesa*, you stink of fire!' I explain that . . . that I went to see Mandela. Why? Because he wants to know what the ANC should be doing to have greater access to whites, er, to offset their irrational fear . . . And as I wrote that open letter asking him to lead forcefully I couldn't refuse to go and see him. Where? Ah, out the Clifton way, he's got a millionaire friend who owns a bungalow there by the sea, these stinking rich white Anglos who suck up to the government-in-waiting. Then? Ah, um, we had a *braaivleis* . . . Windy weather, they didn't do it properly, ah-ah, you know the blacks don't know how to make a fire to barbecue meat. It was probably quieter on the Strandfontein side of the mountain, but that's for the poor people. And? Oh, eh, you know, we drank too much . . . Went for a midnight swim. Bloody cold, the water. I think that's why the voice is so hoarse, maybe a cold coming . . . And? . . . And, uh, the bottle broke. Slippery rocks. By the way, Nelson sends his regards.

She bandages my hand and puts me to bed.

P.S. A few days later we're off to Europe. Just before departing there's a phone call from Mrs Fox. She says some bizarre things have been happening out at Paradise House. A huge bird must have flown into the front window, there were feathers and blood on the stoep. The storm broke some branches in the old bluegum tree. Part of the mountainside burnt down, probably the work of vandals and squatters. But we mustn't worry, our miniature windmill is still safe with her. And police found another half-burnt corpse on the Strandfontein beach. Been 'necklaced'. A victim of political violence. She wishes us a safe journey back.

Othering

Many images remained of that trip, some were strange and deep. Afterwards it was difficult to fit them in a retrievable pattern and it would make no sense to try. Now they are relics or vestiges, instant clichés lifted from their background, studied, discarded.

I remember how we crossed a long-distance truck coming down the mountain pass, with a whoosh of air; in the cabin next to the driver sat a huge naked woman with very big pale bulging breasts. It was a hot day. On the west coast we reached the end of the world: a poor fishing village smothered in fog; the people who seemed to belong to the whitewashed cottages were watching the ocean's hearsay with a mixture of hunger and apprehension. Towards dusk of another afternoon slanted rays lit up a desolate stretch of country as if illuminating it from behind and there were curious plants like cut-outs on the skyline, about two metres high and looking like advancing humans; 'half-people' they were called (*Pachypodium namaquanum*); their red-tipped yellow flowers were always turned northward. In the vicinity of a tiny hamlet known as Dagbreek (Dawn) we saw, off to one side in a peaceful meadow, a house on fire; it was burning majestically without any audible sound in a flowering of sparks and yellow and red flames, spurting tongues through the roof, and there was nobody else for miles around. Once we saw a walled graveyard with only three graves on a barren hillside reaching for blue infinity. On the edge of the desert in the depth of night my last surviving aunt – an old lady of eighty – played music for us on a small electric harmonium; her eyes were blue and she sang and a cloud of mosquitoes silently sifted down to expire on the floorboards; her old husband sat keeping time in an armchair, the lamplight providing him with two silver scales where his eyeglasses might have been. I left her a note to deliver to my mother in heaven.

Some encounters were the continuation, strange and deep, of earlier relationships. It was then as if nothing had happened in the meantime.

When I was young some friends and I often escaped to the Cedarberg mountains to hike for a few days through rugged ravines and along high trails. It was good to feel and smell the earth under our feet. At night we'd sleep in the open. First there'd be the evening fire and laughter and drinking, then when the flames had died down to a palpable black silence one could pluck the stars, and dream.

> Found the path once more
> curling around the hill
> to moon's burial circle
> in a field of herbs
> and the white smell of dead mouths

Our guide was an old initiator named Frederik Joubert, a 'white coloured' who'd lived in the mountains all his life. With his pack donkeys carrying our gear he would take us into the secret passages of endless space. He knew everything and he never tired and he whistled tuneless songs.

Many years had passed. The country out there had changed and we were no longer young. On the trip I'm writing about now – the one which is still flapping through my mind like a broken reel – we entered the mountains again as if going into a book too big to be read. A friend of my youth (I'll call him Dog) took us in, Lady One and I. We'd invited a French couple along. Oom (Uncle) Frederik was waiting at base camp like he used to. He was still old, he now had no teeth, so that the laughter lines down his cheeks were more accentuated, he wore an incongruous little city hat of leather pulled low over his forehead and, as ever, sturdy *velskoene* (raw-hide shoes) without socks; he already had a fire going.

That night it started raining. Our foreign guests were shivering with a wet miserableness and we had to bring out blankets for them. When Oom Frederik emptied his tin mug of wine in a big red mouth it went *glug-glug-glug* down his throat. We slept in our pitched tents; Oom Frederik parcelled himself in a plastic sheet and crawled into a bush with his hat and shoes on.

The morning was soaked through under a clear sky. We moved about stiffly looking for sun-warmed spots. And did Oom Frederik get wet? No, no, he assured us. A hand-sized fire was eating sticks with a cracking sound, his hat was firmly in place, the plastic sheet was still around his shoulders, in the billy the coffee-water was burbling. We weren't going to venture far that day, most French have unfamiliarized European feet. Later on rainbows would be spouting wet fires from the valleys.

He'd have liked to take us walk-about into the recesses of the rocky fastness but he was no longer allowed to use his asses. The Forestry Department had decreed that his animals would bring outlandish seeds into this protected area. He still owned four, he paid a farmer two Rand a month to have them graze on his land. They were getting *onkennig* (unfamiliar, wild and stubborn).

Oom Frederick had been born in a ravine named Wyserskloof, his poor family lived on ground belonging to a white farmer; they cleared the area and tilled the fertile soil, and the owner, seeing that it was good, told them to pack up and move, he chased them away because he wanted to install his son on tamed land. So they crossed the first mountain to Driehoek, where they lived in *klipgatte* ('stone holes'). In the old days they could still eke out a living from the cedar trees, from time to time they chopped down an old one, adzed it and sledged it down the slopes, and they also buried their own dead in coffins made from the fragrant wood which would embalm the discarded husk thus lowered into 'that place where people are saved for nothing'.

There was a hollow not far off, which served as a graveyard; the cedars came there to die and the white skeletons, like time's discarded teeth, were scattered over a large area.

Dog and I had walked these mountains, led by Oom Frederik, in all kinds of weather, as far as the wild wind's most inaccessible lurking places. On occasion we were cut off for days by thick rain, we sheltered within the walls of an abandoned stable and tried in vain to start up a fire under a dripping roof, we survived on brandy and water, for warmth we lay down on a pile of horse dung, and swallows, wearing glistening tailcoats of wetness, came to sit on our faces.

When the wood was damp like today, and when it smoked, Oom Frederik would say it was mourning, and lift a protective hand to his eyes. His older brother Kerneels had lost his seeing – but he, Frederik, had witnessed wonderful things. Once he even beheld the sea. 'It moves! But where is the eye from which the water wells up? Where is the heart of the fountain which fills that dam? Where the opposite bank? I just sat there and I looked, and it was beautiful unto me.'

He nearly drowned one time. He'd drunk far of the vine's ox-blood, the liquid going *glug-glug-glug* down his gullet, it was night, he had to fetch water for coffee, the river was over there towards Middelberg, and so he followed his torch's beam until he arrived at the water's edge, and he put one hand on a log to lean down with the billycan, and the log swam away, 'the world buckled under me', and he fell in and nearly disappeared, his 'upper pants' and under-pants well-versed with water. Was it cold? But no, no, he survived.

Sometimes one just has to wash. Like when you've tangled with a baboon. There are two kinds of baboons — those with round faces and the others with long ones. 'No, *meneer*, the one with the narrow face is an ugly beast, its eyes are so close together. Look, you can't touch him. If you do you are covered in clay. Yes, he shits all over you. Where he gets all that shit from I don't know. And now you can better go wash yourself, or swim. Just you scare him and see the way he shits . . .'

He tilted his head to listen to an insect. 'That's *langasem* (long breath). When that cricket stops shouting it means heavy weather rising. He mustn't tease us so. He's anyway all spongy. Heavy weather has already struck fire in many places.' (I thought of the rainbows.) He had enjoyed the night before very much, never expected to experience such a pleasant evening again. But the French, those people with their 'deaf language! You can see from their faces they don't speak Afrikaans.'

It happened that Dog had him visit the city. A lorry picked him up at the crossroads in a far-away valley where a journey would sometimes sing into the distance, he had his little rucksack, his rolled blanket, his billy. In the city he took all the buildings for hospitals. Couldn't understand why people didn't keep a goat for milk, why they didn't grow vegetables in all those lovely big gardens. In the house of his benefactor he was ill at ease, one wasn't even supposed to spit out the bones on the rug. He saw television and his eyes didn't credit what they saw. There was a programme on Somalia, showing a guide taking a train of donkeys into the savanna. Oom Frederik went to bed while Dog was still drowning the night. He wanted to be ready for an early start. The next day before first light he knocked up his host and asked whether Forestry had phoned. Why? 'No, those people of last night must be lost, we better go find them, the *kaffir* doesn't know the mountains and his donkeys were packed all wrong.'

Mountain people could be dishonest. The farmer would have sheep at home, fattening them with *mealies* and such, they'd be for slaughter. And the labourers would come under the cover of darkness and take one and stab it with a nail, 'right here'; the marrow would be broken and there would be no blood. Early next day when the animal lies dead they would say: '*Baas, Baas* must come look, the sheep lies dead.' And the farmer would say: 'Piet Bloubroek, or Bottelkop, or Hamteef – that thing we must bury. We don't know what ailed it. Maybe the snake bit it.' But they would say: 'No, but *Baas*, we use him. The poison will boil out. Just boil him and the poison will die.' Had I ever tasted a *karmenaadjie* (rib-chop), Oom Frederik wanted to know, one eyelid folded tight against the tear-choked smoke.

On that Sunday morning a religious service was being held for some campers a few hundred yards from our tents and our fire. The voices, lingering with heartfelt despair over psalm and hymn, floated away up the valley. Heads were bowed, people closed their eyes the better to see God, a parson in shorts was delivering a sonorous complaint. Dog told of how he attended a service in the cave where the Jouberts live, how the preacher warned against abusing the body, which is a temple of God (blessed be the Memory), and Oom Kerneels had kept one impatient red unseeing eye open during the lengthy prayed lamentation, and when it was over he sighed and took Dog outside and requested him in an urgent whisper to go fetch the you-know-what in his car, because 'this old temple is now as dry as thirst.'

Did Oom Frederik know Dirk Ligter, the legendary fugitive Hottentot from hereabouts? He was still small when Dirk Ligter was already a big man. Here, up this direction (he pointed a hand which was like a dry bird), there was a place called Koorstenberg. An old woman used to live there. A widow. She had a fiddle. Dirk sickened for this fiddle, the old woman didn't want to sell, he insisted, offered her one pound ten shillings, it was *much* money. No, she said. Well, then Dirk Ligter came in the night when she was asleep and he stole the fiddle. Put down one pound and ten shillings for the old body, right there. So the police went after him.

'And the police are on him! So he looks at the police like this and then he just disappears. A quick man!' The police on horseback 'throw their horses in the road.' There went Dirk Ligter. They got to where he'd turned off and there they lost his spoor. 'He had turned himself into an anthill, see.' One policeman climbed on the anthill to scout far and wide for Dirk Ligter. He even unbuttoned his fly and pissed.

They went hunting him again and this time they captured him. They always off-saddled at his late father's *werf* to ask for fodder and 'to hold afternoon'. They were strutting. 'And he's the man who says the police can never catch him. Look there, Joubert, now we got him. There he sits like a long-faced baboon. We have him.' Dirk Ligter only laughed. 'No, *meneer* Joubert,' he explained, 'they're too rotten to catch me.' But it had been getting winter, in these parts the world can bite cold, he'd decided to go home for a while and that was how they'd tracked him down.

His father gave them coffee and bread. They said: 'Well now, Joubert, you treated us well, when you come to Clanwilliam you must come to us and we'll give you a cool drink.' What could Dirk Ligter give? The man had fuck-all. The man was going to prison. So Oom Frederik's late pa spoke: 'Let him play the fiddle a little.' And he played the fiddle. When that man played the police danced.

Then Dirk Ligter said: 'No, *meneer* Joubert, they are too feeble, we shall make a joke. Look, now they have their horses and I walk on foot. Let me show you my speed!'

The road curved away around the *kraal* where the moon used to be buried with a dark mouth. God knows (sacred is the Name), when the police reached the enclosure Dirk Ligter was already up the hill, and he was manacled! He shouted: 'A good day to you, *meneer* Joubert! There they come now!'

Oh, he ran away from those horses. That same day, when the police finally galloped into Clanwilliam, and the froth from their horses' flanks had flecked their shins, Dirk Ligter was already sitting on the police station's roof. He was singing: 'They are still coming. They came to fetch me and I'm already here.'

Another time Dirk Ligter had to look after a farmer's donkeys. It was at Welbedag where the bushes grow thick. A mountain-hare lived in the thickets there, of the grey kind that can run as fast as death. The farmer had said: 'Dirk, there's an easel here that must multiply. If she multiplies, don't let the foal get hurt or left behind.'

Well then, he went with the span of donkeys through that way. And the rock-hare jumped out. And Dirk Ligter said: 'Hee-haw-hee, here's your mummy, hee-haw-hee!' Thus the man shouted, the pregnant mare shouted, the hare tried to get away, this way and there, it didn't do any good, Dirk Ligter was heading him off. He kept the hare among the asses. The hare tried bolting this way, escaping that way, Dirk Ligter brought him back, and a scrub hare is a rapid beast, for doesn't he sprint like a corkscrew of lightning?

And that evening he had him in the chicken-wire enclosure among the donkeys. Now the hare sat there in a corner all folded up small, terrified, going hee-haw with a squeaky voice. Farmer asked: 'Dirk, did the mare get more then?' Dirk Ligter said: '*Ja, Baas*, but the filly was bloody difficult.'

Then Oom Frederik looked at me. To him who saw no boundary between the now of reality and the then where stories wormed through the words, I had been with him in those mountains more often than I could know of. He even remembered how we'd fallen down the other side of Sneeuberg.

He slowly told us again the story of Sneeuberg. Hans Moller had gone with the others to harvest *buchu* (a medicinal and aromatic shrub), that time when Forestry had given him a permit and the *buchu* fetched such a good price. Oom Frederik was present. They'd climbed up Uitkyk (Lookout) way, through Duiwelsgat (Devil's Hole), until they'd reached Sweetvlak (Perspiration Plain), and down the other side toward the river, steep track. The first night Hans Moller's wife got sick, sicker, sicker. All the other workers ran away. She died.

Then the 'tigers' (leopards) came in the fast darkness, roaring, they couldn't care a damn, they were that hungry. They had smelled the dead wife. Hans Moller built a fire and the stars were embers. The leopards just kept on prowling ever closer.

And so Hans Moller started playing his *vijool* (violin). Right through the night until the next morning he played and the animals were bewitched. The next day he made a coffin for his wife and piled stones all around her. 'For in that place there are stones wherever you may look.' And when he left he took all the other people's *buchu* as well. It was only right. But it had been a bad night.

'If he couldn't play the fiddle, he would now be dead as well.'

P.S. Dog is an imaginary character — or rather, the shaman's disguise. Frederik Joubert is still alive. These incidents he related to me, and to a friend called Saayman.

Africa on My Mind

(Island Notes)

1

To write about Africa is to go on a journey, to be confronted by the endlessly unfolding conjugations of an elusive reality, and you yourself with your hump and your carapace as a shadowy figure among the milling market traders, as a street beggar encountered at night sitting on the haunches in a cone of darkness; it is to travel into a mythical world of invisible forces, of dusty miracles, of taboos and drumtalk and water spirits and court singers and magicians unrolling before you the seamless cloth of witchcraft and 'reality', there to throw the small shells and the knuckle-bones from which the past will be read as drawn into the future; it is to embark on travels into a language which is matter, an exorcism of time, the dance movements of the tongue living in the grave.

2

Often – when thinking about it or travelling through parts of it or staying put to watch the movements and feel the emptiness (there is always the beckoning of emptiness behind closed eyelids throbbing like the distant heart of a drum) – the question arises: how to write *about* Africa? From what angle? From what background? Can it be done? Mentioning *Africa* instantly brings to the fore either one of two discourses. Seen from the outside, from the north (which is also the norm), the thinkthing resembles a kind of big black bag into which everything disappears. You know it must contain unimaginable loot and incomprehensible cult artefacts. You suspect it holds something like a genetic pool of bygone forms of knowledge which should be preserved (because we don't wish to amputate the unknown past so as not to foreclose any options), and maybe artificially cultivated, as is done with rare species in a zoo, although no longer of any application in the real world. Africa is a luxury item in the antique store of the mind. Until recently the dominant opinion in Europe was that Africans constitute the mysterious but well-worn link between animal and man. Africa is supposed to be the living proof of evolutionary doctrine, the blind fumbling which postulates that man started somewhere standing up on his hindlegs to develop the knack of shitting on his shoes. And because there was a start, isn't man therefore ineluctably doomed to end? This is the metaphysical regression brought about by the notion of progress, that mad sadness when we tumbled from knowing into the need to understand. And we have from this severance the infinite variations of white alienation making Africa the back-broken object of its fears and desires. Even well-meaning observers prefer to see the continent as one big black heart allowing for the projection of illicit expectations, ah, sweet terror, and the vicarious thrill (is the heart not a bag?) of being bitten if you were to put your hand inside, to bring back 'home' an exotic disease. Or the second discourse, which rises from within through throats swollen with demagogical crap, giving us scraps of 'unity' and 'independence', shifting the blame, accepting no responsibility, feeding off the guilty consciences of liberal whites, dancing and beating drums for the white man, bidding for a position of dependence that could be remunerated. How does one break through to the infinitely subtle nuances of people, so different from one region to the other, dying and living and dying? Maybe it can only be done in fragmentary fashion. Africa must be written — and not to please the masters of culture living in London and Paris. This is a project for Unesco: to bring the continent to an intelligible surface of flesh and blood, fifty writers (from inside and outside) must be sent there for three years, just to weave a map of words as wrapping for yams and stumps.

3

According to Olfert Dapper, the seventeenth-century Dutch chronicler who wrote a definitive description of Africa without ever leaving his native land of polders and canals, the name is of Greek origin. Other Greek names for the continent on the outer rim of imagination were *Olympia, Oceania, Coriphe, Hesperia, Ammonide, Ethiopia, Cyrene, Ofiuse, Cephenia, Erie.* The Latins (he said) knew it as either *Libya* — from the daughter of Epaphus, the son of Jupiter — or

Africa, deduced from Afer, the son of Hercules the Libyan. The Moors called it *Alkebulan* and the Indians *Bezecath*. The Arabs knew the continent as *Ifiriquie*, from *Faruch* meaning 'something apart' (according to Thevet). But Marmol holds that the Arab word *Ifiriquie* came into being after the name of an Arab king, Melek Ifiriquie, who took his army to populate areas known as *Magribou* or *Magrip*. Other ancient authors (summoned by Mr Dapper) claim the word as being of Hebrew origin, from *Aphar* meaning 'dust'. But to Bochart the root must have been Phoenician, from *Feruch* — 'ear of corn'. There was already a lot of corn and dust in Barbary.

4

It is the season of dust. Sometimes, with a bit of luck, and then not every year, a wind rises and the sky loses its white breath. The palm trees make awkward noises, surprised that they still know how to dance. People hereabouts call this winter. The evenings are cool. In the living-room, there's a clay pot with incandescent coals. Incense — *churai* — is put on the coals and a pleasant glow and aroma fill the room. At night I wake as if on board a schooner and watch the moon white and bloated behind the garden's waving branches. The sea is blinding. (Or the imagination, a future existing without any change since all time, which you don't see because you lie with closed eyelids in a dark room behind walls giving on a garden full of rocking sounds and patterns of darkness.) Wind has blown away the *imam*'s call to prayer, but in an inner courtyard behind a wall a cock is loudly pacing his territory and enumerating his steps and his dire imprecations. In the early morning I go for a run — through narrow lanes where bunches of purple and red and white and orange bougainvillaea peep over the walls, along the sea's leak where brightly patterned *pirogues* lie beached above the damp reach of high tide, up the hill as far as the massive ramparts of the ruined fort where young mystics now grow tomatoes and runner beans and play their drums and sell drugs. A big cargo steamer is anchored on the vaporous mirror of water. The wind brings faint trumpet sounds. I look down the steep walls to where waves splash a spray over black basalt rocks. Angelo Mosca, the unbelievably corpulent Italian married to a tiny woman from Casamance, is sitting all alone on a rock, the wind is using his billowing and copious yellow garb as bellows, he is blowing his trombone. Suddenly the sun strikes a golden eye-flash from his instrument. Sulei says that when they go out to fish on a Sunday, and should Angelo accidentally fall overboard, he is too heavy to be hauled in so that they have to tow him back to port tied to the stern.

5

Our memories are rubbed raw, and there's nothing we can do about it. Our experiences are bitter, and of no use. No victory, no advance, just an ongoing life, the continuation of giving a little and taking a little, a *connection* where the smallest initiative becomes a *mechanism* for running down, stripping, redistributing, sharing, profit- ing. There is no accumulation, no planning, no fashioning of the future, except where the projection of an illusion is used as a technique to irrigate the immediate present. No anticipation. Why? Because the continent has been done out of its history, deprived of the possibility to define its own future and directions at a critical juncture in the world's development – when there was industrializa- tion, the separation of church and state, the creation of welfare systems, modernization. The dispossession of Africa was a factor in speeding up that development in Europe and North America, to a lesser extent in Asia. And simultaneously: traditional support net- works treat all needs as equally important, function as means of distribution, making it impossible for the individual to rise above his peers through selection or elimination or private initiative. The incentive is for sharing, not gathering. Why is it said that only the strong survive in Africa? Because it is expected of the strong to look after the needs of his dependants, and the weak tie him down and make him strong – through presents, by voting for him and working for him; it is in this context that concepts such as 'corrup- tion' and 'ethics' must be seen. The state is there only to be cut up and parcelled out, functionaries are suited and perfumed rats with the power to distribute. All the problems have been envisaged, all solutions understood. This will bring no forward movement. The brilliant indictment proffered by intellectuals, politicians and ad- ministrators has a paralysing effect because it always puts them in the impotent stance of victims. A historically correct reading will at the same time be totally false since it can draw no line from cause to effect to action. Blame us on history, and history is white invention.

6

He has been living for many years on this island. It's not quite clear where he originally came from. Maybe his family were refugees, all exterminated in a death camp except for a far-away cousin; maybe he was the black sheep of rich parents, maybe an illegitimate offspring who ran away to Africa in desperation or out of idealism. With time he adapted well to local conditions, becoming subtle and devious, conscious of the primary importance of public appearances, learning, too, that all relations are based on the barter system and that prolonged negotiations are more important than concluding transactions, but also that all plans and projects will disappear in the sand. And that it is good to keep an eye on the sea while waiting to die. Only rarely, like an old fever flaring up unexpectedly, was there the sharp desire to win back something of a lost world. Today, for the *Korité* feast celebrating the end of *Ramadan*, when a trustworthy man accompanied by three honourable witnesses saw the new moon horning the horizon, and the news was spread and extensive festive meals were prepared and old and young donned their fanciest garments, today he, too, put on an embroidered *boubou* and new sandals and strolled through the town to congratulate everybody.

In the strait between island and mainland coast there were swarms of birds and in places the sea boiled. Tunnyfish were hunting schools of smaller fare; it was this exuberant plundering and feeding that drew the birds. Sometimes you could see the tunny diving in arcs, sharp and wet like the vicious fighting of an army of swordsmen in the water. The man's paramour, a local lady, wore a shimmering dress and an exquisitely scented headscarf and her prettiest jewels around the throat. It was the chance, as on any number of other occasions, for people to exchange money and gifts and food, and thus to lend a new impetus to the never-ending process of giving and receiving. The shutters of the man's house were open so that all could look in. The house showed signs of neglect caused by seawind and damp. All of a sudden, the man appeared dressed in *toubab* clothes with tie and laced-up shoes. He obliged his concubine, resigned to his sudden moods, to also put on a white woman's frock, with handbag and high-heeled shoes. The woman, normally so bewitching, appeared ill at ease and stupid in this foreign harness. The man insisted on a Western meal. On the table there were candles and he poured red wine in glasses. Then he put a record of classical music on the player, turned up the volume to earsplitting level so that sounds flooded the island, and closed his eyes. In the sandy lane below the windows of the house a group of urchins gathered, clapped their hands in rhythm to the sonata and made up words in their own language to accompany the notes. Over the sea the sun died red in the haze and the smoke of distance.

7

My friend, the writer from the Low Countries – we call him the Flying Dutchman but his true name is Daidai – has been living for two months in Sulei's house on the island. He often sings and he eats peanuts which he buys from Aliou's grandmother down by the waterfront, and he works as if possessed. In the mornings he comes with the scribbled sheets of night's labour and we dissect those. By noon he has already destroyed the cadences and the colours and now he tears at his curls. He seems incapable of pointing his African book in the right direction, he wants to draw in too many divergent themes at the same time, he is unsure of the narrator's position. In the late afternoon, when wind sometimes hoists its sail, we go down to the port and take our seats at a rickety table outside the Au St Germain, Rehena's café. (Rehena is a Catholic, she tore a full-colour picture of President Diouf from a magazine and pasted it on her door, she is also the local guide who can tell you everything about the island; just after daybreak her brother sprints around and around the whispering of the sea's lips, together with a few others he is practising for the annual marathon, he enjoys leaving me standing and winded.) We order *mazout* (whisky and coke) and chew our reflections in leisurely movements. Africa is inevitably a breeding ground of fantasies, that's why it is so arduous to tie it down in writing. There's always the temptation to use it as an exotic circumstance, a background against which the lone pilgrim (European) can play out his existential searchings. When the white man came to Africa it was with a head stuffed with descriptions of the unknown; actually these were only projections of some buried consciousness: Monomotapa, the unicorn, women with their breasts sliced off, talking baboons. You always find what you expect to find – after all, one *creates* reality. On top of that there are so many mentally deranged characters, white and black. For a long time a young French demoiselle, working in the local embassy, made a regular weekly trip to the island. Quite prettily clothed in a short black dress she was. Long brown legs. Then, at sundown, on the sandy square next to the market stalls under the big baobab, she always squatted down in the same spot, her arms wrapped tightly around the knees, and commenced howling in the most horrifying fashion . . . Le capitaine Walker is a mythomaniac erring through the alleys. If you run into him he always pretends to be hurrying somewhere fixed with a single mind. He is slightly light of pigmentation and imagines himself to be a 'racially pure' Frenchman. His elder brother had served the colonial administration, went mad and died young. Gradually le capitaine Walker took over his departed brother's stories, unearthed the latter's medals and pinned them to his chest. Now his past is that of his brother . . . Sometimes Ka'afir suddenly rears up before you, stark naked, or perhaps sporting only a female's panties and high heels. He is the child of old Mame Louise, the most senior inhabitant who has pale milk in her eyes. Here at the very same Au St Germain, Ka'afir once stopped at Daidai's table, pulled down his shorts, took hold of his penis and slapped it on the table-top as if he wanted to sell a dark fish . . . No, the Flying Dutchman decides, he will let go of this ambitious African novel. It has become too much of a labyrinth. One can get lost in such a continent. Perhaps it will be simpler to construct a story around Comtesse Delafesse, the American expatriate. She must have a rich and improbable past. She speaks such a fractured language. Each year she will fast with her local Muslim friends even though she herself is not a believer. Together with them she will then later slaughter the sacrificial goat. She has a black lover, an elderly fisherman, who comes to visit her every Sunday with a blue thing from the depths wrapped in his trousers. Then they darken the house and go lie on the bed of sighs and slow movements. It is also a way of killing goat. We munch some more peanuts and order a second round of *mazout* and agree that Comtesse Delafesse ought actually to be called Ms Bumhill.

8

To continue writing Africa: an image haunts you. This island was created layer upon layer, demolished, rebuilt. At the end of one sandy lane heading for the sea there are a number of steps, you climb to a concrete platform which quite evidently has neither history nor purpose, a balcony jutting above the languid water. At night there is another, earlier life on the island. Wind goes about wearing a sombre cloak and where he goes he leaves ripples on the water with the colour of silver oil. From the courtyards, from behind closed shutters over windows without glass, from rooms with peeling walls there emerges a murmur, a goat grunts a ruminated comment. Wraiths move through the darkness as shades relieved of their diurnal aspect. Last night until four o'clock there was a service in the mosque. *Ramadan*, the month of fasting, is nearly over. The faithful are permitted to eat only after a given hour at night or at a specified time hard before sunrise. During the day they take nothing, not even water. But at set moments they will produce a plastic bottle of cool water from somewhere and refresh the ankles, feet, hands, neck, face and ears, and dip a finger in the water to brush teeth and gums without swallowing as much as a single drop. Now, as they approach the end of this period of abstinence, they redouble the pietistic recital of verses and prayers ... It is hard to pin down this island — like wind in the palm trees, the same wind (*harmattan*) which veils the horizon in a luminous white haze of dust so that you can no longer perceive the continent with Dakar's silhouette. The island belongs to everybody and to no one. It is in an unremitting process of self-incineration. But this implosion, as much a form of survival, creates spaces. Gaps and holes abound. Why does one sleep restlessly? Where do all these feverish dreams originate? Why is there this island delirium? There is that which is indigenous to the place — its weighted history (like a dust-laden glowing wind above us), the shifting nature of its constituent components (population, authority, ownership), the fact that it lives turned in upon itself and at the same time exposed to the maggots who at regular intervals wash ashore from the *chaloupe*, with pinked skins and dark glasses and cameras, and then a section of the local populace will ritualistically gnaw at the tourists. Who is watching whom? Who the gawker and who the performer? But there are other, more mysterious openings. For instance, the absence of a daily social behaviour which would have filled your time elsewhere. Perhaps, too, it is in the fleeting and ritualistic communion with the locals, the recitations which you mime, the benedictory fingers over the heart, the white of teeth, briefly caressing the other's palms, and that all of this is matter without content, ceaselessly repeated in arabesques. Then you lie awake in the morning with all the spaces and absences and hollows between things, and you listen to the senseless screamed matins of the cock, and you reflect upon the fact that all the people here have variations on the same name, and you sob without knowing why, perhaps a profound blank or void, a strange fear and longing for the soughing oblivion of an infinitely immobile trajectory, where you hail from and which awaits you, and it is as if you were cornered with yourself. Like having to piggy-back your own corpse across the stream of death, and it is growing heavier, and half-way to the other side the arms are tightening around your neck ... Just above the sea-wall there's a site a few steps away from the pergola with the chairs and the tables, by day many people pass over this spot of earth but at night it is deserted and cool. In the wee hours of darkness a dog comes and starts pawing. Later on the sand turns moist. And then he uncovers the dead body of a girl. It is the cadaver of someone who must have been fourteen years old, after local custom wound in a shroud only. The dog sniffs at the corpse, licks clean the face, perhaps commits other unmentionable deeds as well. Then, when a spark of the immanent day starts glowing, he covers the dead once more. Nobody knows how long this had been going on and nobody will speak about it in the open. The miracle is that the corpse has remained unblemished. Perhaps there's some substance in the sand, a mineral or a chemical which inhibits decomposition. Moussa is the name of the old night watchman with long caftan and fez and with white mucus in the corners of his eyes who hunkers down the whole night long over a tin of live coals by the side-entrance to the hotel. A low protection of cardboard boxes makes his squat a little more private. When the dog doesn't turn up for several nights in a row he starts surreptitiously scooping away the sand. Down below in the hole he finds the corpse. The shroud is gone. Next to the cadaver the dog lies, all caked in sand, alive, making small whimpering noises in the throat.

Gorée, March 1993

The Shattered Dream

'Le principal, c'est d'emmerder les autres,
sans qu'ils sachent pourquoi.'
Luis Buñuel

First of all I must indicate what I am not.

I'm not an academic — that is, I have little or no formal training in the history and theory of literature, and neither talent nor interest for the noble art of teaching. I am not a theorist, although it is clear that theories can help elucidate if not actually shape the discipline one is involved in. But then, in the effort to unravel understanding, one theory is as good as the next as far as I'm concerned. In fact, I'm not sure that it is necessary to *understand* writing. The word 'understand' already carries within it, on most European tongues, the notion of arrest, of immobility.

I'm not an analyst. Naturally, when a 'field of being' works for me — this could be a text or a visual work — when it hooks or provokes my attention, further triggering emotions and reactions which may be instinctive and/or acquired, when it involves me at the risk of leading me where I don't want to go, then I'm as interested as the next person in the what and the how of its workings. Perhaps even in the why of it. It is obvious that the effectiveness of a given work can be explained, to some extent, by recognizing the means employed: the structure, the rhythms, the texture, the colours, the gambolling gamut and gammon of associations, the etc. But for me the dissection of a work, its deconstruction in order to apprehend and reconstruct areas of comprehension — these are more often than not baroque decorations of the mind, a kind of stultifying movement which masks the starker confrontation with the image or the shadow of the thing of being.

One or two of the people present here who know me only too well will tell you it is my habit to provoke my audience by being 'different' or indifferent or 'difficult' or insulting. They will inform you that I have a penchant for spitting in the soup. Please don't get me wrong. I'm not passing judgement on you. We need university lecturers to keep the so-called creative sectors of society within bounds and to limit the unemployed on the streets. Besides, I'm as much of a crook as the next guy: I also finger and pocket perceptions, using the specifics of the craft, with the intention of manipulating attitudes.

The act of writing or painting is an attempt at communication. If we temporarily leave out of consideration the desire for communicating with the gods or the ancestors, and if we discard the solitary pleasure of communicating with the self, peeling back the skins of the known in the hope of discovering the subcutaneous unknown, then we are left with the practice of presenting the products of our making to reader and onlooker. To transmit what? Meaning? Belief? Opinion? Judgement? Question? Indignation? Beauty? And to whom? The people? The believers? The hyenas? The princes and bosses? And again, why? And then again, how?

To write or to paint is an individual activity, and yet it can only be completed by being shared or handed over to the consumer. Samuel Beckett says that the work which is not submitted to the appraisal of others will pass away in horrible agony. When a work is considered pure creation and when its function is stilled at birth, it is doomed to nothingness. It can of course also be argued that a work which *is* seen or read by others is in a permanent condition of incompleteness because each new consumer will add to or subtract from the reach of the object – unless the expert interpreters succeed in limiting its meaning once and for all. *Lie there and don't move!*

You will notice that I keep mentioning painting as well as writing. This is because for a pastime I indulge in both; it has been my experience that there are many correspondences between the two disciplines and that it can be enriching to read the one in the light of the other. Furthermore, since this is a get-together of satraps and savants who walk around with reference libraries in their heads, I have decided to give my credibility some weight by inviting aboard my paper two books. The one is Samuel Beckett's *Le monde et le pantalon (The World and Pants)* – written in 1945 as an introduction to an exhibition of paintings by the brothers Bram and Geert van Velde (I don't know whether it exists in English as well); and the other is written by François Cheng and called *Vide et Plein* meaning, I suppose, *Empty and Full*, though I'm tempted to translate it as *Void and Avoid.* In typically post-modernist fashion I shall steal and forge, as martext and castigator and adulterator I shall sub-textuate.

Despite the thanatoid opposition between tradition and modernism — to which I shall return later — all creative activity always involves telling a story. Even just exhibiting the elements and the tools of telling constitutes a story. With words you cannot help but tell yourself, building from dying matter a wall against extinction, or throwing them out like birds to go and scout for an emerging continent. Here I want to tell you a story.

On a recent visit to South Africa (Nowhere Land, Utopia) my wife and I once stopped where a mountain pass peaked in the blue sky. It was a clear, windless day. We had with us in the car another gentleman, I shall call him Mr X. He got out, looked up to heaven with his hands cupped around his mouth, and shouted, 'Hey, you go-o-o-o-ds! You are all de-e-e-ead!' When he returned to the car he winked at us and said: 'You know, I could hear the echoes come up from the valley — dead-dead-dead-dead . . .'

When a fool trespasses upon the terrain of experts such as yourselves, there is always the risk that he may provoke the wrong echoes in his use of conceptions you are familiar with. I shall try to fool you some more by spelling out what I think I do. As I move along I hope these reflections worn smooth by constant contemplation will be seen as not entirely unrelated to the subject of tradition and modernism which I've been summoned to address. It is after all in the process of positioning yourself that you define the playing field.

Classical Chinese philosophy would seem to be posited on the difficulty of holding in equilibrium an apparent contradiction: the universe is completed and unchanging; and, the universe is being created continuously. Let me jump to another register. Death is our common destiny, but this knowledge is so all-pervasive as to annul itself. (And how could there be death unless we know about it?) Life then is the fleshing out of death. It could be argued that painting and poetry are the gestures and the breath partaking of the creation of the universe. In other words, creating the harmony which already exists. The definite (or the definitive) is always for tomorrow. We are free slaves to the incomplete nature of awareness. (And the hand which writes is a thief.)

Again I quote Beckett: 'Whenever we want words to overflow or outflank, when we intend to express something else than mere words, they line up in such a fashion as to cancel themselves out. That, undoubtedly, is what gives life its charm ... For we are not talking about knowing, but about vision, a pointing of view! And a pointing of view in the only field which sometimes allows itself to be seen as it is, which doesn't always insist upon being badly known, which may grant the faithful the privilege of ignoring all that which is not appearance: the interior field.'

The image, unclothed by understanding or even meaning, cannot be fixed. It moves against the dullness of information. It is movement. It is metaphor. It is detonation. The aim is not to survive, but to keep one jump (or possibility) ahead of the deadening hand of the state of reasonable understanding. Obviously, to interact (or to seduce) there must be at least a partial slotting in with the recognizable codes – to keep moving the image must set off resonances. But, and this is a pointer towards what I consider modernism to be, I'm interested in the unbalancing act upon the highwire of fatality strung between life and death.

I'm not for a moment suggesting that this 'image', or sequence of explosions, is buried in some eternity inside yourself and that creative life is a long slog to crack open the clichés so that the images may emerge. They are there for the taking and may pop up in the most humdrum places. While preparing this contribution, for instance, I quite accidentally came across the following headlines in two issues of *The Independent*, respectively of 3 June and 11 June, and each item might have been a way of getting behind expectation to startling possibilities. I give them to you at random: 'My brilliant career on the bottle', or 'A torn penis is an emergency', or 'Darkness that will shed new light', or 'Virtual reality realised', or/and 'Simulated sex lacks the human touch', or 'Naked man dies in street chase arrest', or 'Macbeth finds comfort and joy in Olympic creed', or 'Poverty as pornography', or 'An epidemic of meaninglessness'.

The amateur should be warned against the notion of aesthetic hierarchy. Since poems or paintings are not sausages, one cannot think of them as being good or bad. At most one can say they translate absurd and mysterious attempts at getting at the image (*magie*), losing more or less along the way, and that they are less or more effective at mouthing internal tensions. You, as outsider, cannot judge the adequacy since you are not in the skin of the stretched one; besides, loss and gain are immaterial in the economy of art where the unsaid is the light of the said (or where the expressed is the shadow of the unexpressed), and all presence is absence. 'Truth, at any rate, is but to collect a fart of the largest number of people.'

Where is the heart of the matter? Before, long ago, we were inventing ourselves through stories. Then we put up with ourselves by means of history: the *reading* of stories. It was fondly assumed that history had a meaning, that it must *make* sense. Even a mite of time, we thought, will anagrammatically emit an item of grammar. There are of course many characteristics of tradition which gave shape to this dream. Thus it could be said that there'd be no modernism without tradition.

For me tradition and modernism cannot be opposed in time, at least not in the accepted sense of 'before' and 'after'. There were modernists many centuries ago. In the times of tradition, though, time must have been palpable. Isn't traditionalism also an approach to stopping time by attempting to picture and present it? Tradition permitted a working and reworking of memory within a scope of fairly fixed references and a hierarchy of values. These references were known widely enough for you to be comprehensible: you knew how man and the world were created, power flowed from the top down and when you had existential *Angst* you sorted it out with the old man on the mountain. (Later, Freud would diffuse the equation by having carnal knowledge of the begetter and submerging the mountain in some romantic Utopia signposted as the 'subconscious', but he was just a fool writer who wanted to be a scientist.) Things painted and truths stated were objective because you yourself were an object within a fixed pattern. The word was magical because it came from the mouth and understanding your life (or, rather, *accepting* it) must have seemed like a never-ending process of mouth-to-mouth resuscitation. But all along the modernists must have been there: people involved with the *feel* of being alive and not necessarily by the *sense* thereof.

Modernism became dominant with the loss of acceptance of a coherent social and intellectual hierarchy and its court of truths. Linear or progressive time, starting from the unknowable to disappear into the unknown, was destroyed. The mirror cracked and images started leaking out. Modernism works on the mechanisms of memory, perception and awareness – in fact, the matter of expression becomes the flesh of consciousness. In modernism we could isolate in its thingness that which we wanted to depict. We could now see in the dark under an empty sky and an immobile earth. We could track new time in the multiple ways in which it moved things, creating new relationships. Modernism wanted to indicate change, to *be* change.

How does one embody change? And, once we realized that nothing is fixed or for ever, was it possible ever again to represent the unchangeable? We became a never-ending succession of moments, images of images of images. The painter or the poet became part of the fleeting process of creating awareness. Now no detail of the work could be finished until such time as the whole was completed. But, paradoxically, because there were no boundaries any more and virtually no attachment to values, everything became static.

Modernism was more than the scarecrow which I'm manipulating here to attract the birds. Let's take it in its broader context. It also embodied the dream of progress of course. In that we were naïve. We thought man had the capacity to change for the better, and these very efforts brought out the worst in him. Was modernism wrecked on the reefs of tradition? Or was the dream of change, improvement, reason, enlightenment, development, justice . . . itself a tyranny that could only lead to alienation?

The Gulf War — was it an expression of modernism or tradition? How did it become possible that it should be 'normal' for a coalition of modern powers to set out deliberately to kill hundreds of thousands — draining the dam to embarrass Saddam the fish? And how did we swallow the lies about Iraq supposedly having 400,000 soldiers massed somewhere? How could we ever pretend to believe that the war was not about controlling the petrol and not made acceptable by our racist sentiments about those murderous fanatic Arabs? How quickly we moved from history to the supposedly 'soft' imperialism of *pax americana*! How can one even conceive of the obscenity of American victory parades with firework displays to re-enact the nights over Baghdad? But, at least, let this much be noted — so I heard on the radio — the stocks and shares of the company providing the confetti rose dramatically.

Let us consider the dream of modernist social development. Where is the Soviet Union? Marxism had become the science of doublethink. Fools that we were! The mother of socialism is now a drunken empire, its foundations destroyed by an accumulation of lies, its scaffolding infested by gangsters. 'Virtual socialism' was a con trick.

The dream is a killer. The dreamers are manipulators who tried to redirect rivers, who blackened the skies and pauperized a continent. Modernism is not the dream, it is the shattering of a dream. We know now that the people can never be the state, that classical and traditional modernism is the struggle between master and subjects, between the citizens and the state. We know that perception will be manipulated to sustain or extend power and that awareness grows through resistance to power. Can there be a modernism, at least in the creative area, which is based on non-power?

And Europe, the black hole of superior selfishness with walls rising ever higher to keep out the poor, the Europe which has international interests and pretensions but no foreign policy – is it not the product of modernism applied to protect traditional privileges? And the Nether World, such as Africa, euphemistically referred to as the Third World, now sinking in the morass of plague diseases and regression and barbarism – what did modernism do for it? The rebels who have taken over Addis Ababa, aren't they but feudal traditionalists with a veneer of modernist vocabulary?

Cut loose from our traditions and unreconstructed by modernism we seem, more and more, to be the alienated and impotent products of a surfeit of manipulated information. We have knowledge – of a kind! – of the unbearable, without being able to influence events. We are being dehumanized because we are exposed to the inhuman without the means to change relationships. We are now well-informed clever fools! Our frustration must lead to nihilism or to decadence.

The dream of modernism lies shattered, even though the shards reflect interesting images. Modernism – in architecture, painting, science . . . – was a way of getting God off man's back; these modes of expression deconstructed into post-modernism, bringing God back to the circus as a crippled clown to prattle parrot texts. Post-modernism, it would seem to me, is posited on three complementary notions: the equal importance of all 'texts', the excision of the author (and the concomitant valorization of the critic or the 'analyst'), a Freudian romanticism where 'sub-conscious' equals 'subtext'.

Perhaps it was inevitable that we should work with margins as mirrors. 'Life,' Blaise Cendrars argued in an essay he wrote for *Der Sturm* on the Douanier Henri Rousseau, 'is the sun which rots.' (And he added: 'The heart is the world's black sun.') We have perhaps already accepted the meaninglessness of so-called higher truths. We take in facts as a collection of dead objects cut off from a larger reality. We slide effortlessly from reality to dream, from fact to fiction to publicity. We do keep an idle interest alive in alternatives to the norm. Frederic Jameson, in his book *Postmodernism*, shows that it is little more than an innovative extension of liberal secularism. The 'innovation' comes in post-modernism's treatment of 'other cultures' and minorities. An appreciation of plurality and active representation of the 'other' is said to be a corner-stone of postmodernist thought. But the 'others' are meaningless, or reduced to spectacle. Jameson ends up by saying that the engine of postmodernism is not some altruistic pursuit of art and culture and tolerance, but market forces. Post-modernism came about because the jaded senses required a renewal of the stock of intellectual objects.

Cervantes describes a painter who when asked what he was painting, answered: 'That which will come from my brush.' Matisse said: 'I continue working until my hand sings.'

And Shih-t'ao, a Chinese painter who lived in the beginning of the Ming dynasty (around the fifteenth century), wrote often of this necessary tension and flow between the specific (or *mountain*) and the void (or *water*). Landscape painting was then known as Mountain-Water. At one point he said: 'The work is not in the brush, just to be transmitted; it is not in the ink, which will make it possible for it to be seen; it is not in the Mountain, which would express immobility nor in the Water which would express its movements; it is not in Antiquity, which would have made it limitless, nor in the Present, which would have allowed it to be without blinkers. Indeed, if the succession of the ages is without disorder and if Brush and Ink can be maintained, it is because they are intimately penetrated by the work. The work, in truth, reposes on the principles of Discipline and of Life: by the One multiplicity is mastered; from Multiplicity to master the One. The work doesn't have to have recourse to Mountain or Water or Brush or Ink. Neither to the ancients nor to the moderns or the saints. It is the veritable work, that which is founded on its own substance.'

And in a poem written in the (unpainted) void of a painting, he jotted: 'In the old days Ku K'ai-chih attained the Triple Perfection, it is claimed. As for me, I have reached the three follies: mad am I, mad my language, mad my painting. I'm still looking for the way to true madness though.'

We, in the Nether World particularly, are responsible for ourselves. It is up to us to turn death around — also that death of the mind — so as to make living more dignified and worthwhile. For this we have to keep on labouring the void.

It has perhaps been too easy (especially since I shirked the subject I was expected to talk about) and somewhat unfair to attack you by assuming that you are old-fashioned modernist dreamers or post-modernist mindgame players. If I made you feel a little guilty, don't worry — I've become a bit of a preacher. And anyway, you intellectuals are guilty by definition.

I'd like to end with an upbeat note — Adorno saying: 'We must take all the arguments developed by romantic thinking or the reactions against Western civilization, and put it to the service of a new age of Reason.'

Essen, June 1991

Dog's Bone

'A man with a wooden nose knows
it can do no good to sniff at axes.'

*Ka'afir**

'When a goat is present it is stupid
to bleat in its place.'

*Ahmadou Hampaté-Bâ**

I can just about describe myself as an alumnus of the University of South Africa here in Pretoria. Years ago, when I shied my time away in the shade of Maximum Security wing, on a hillock just outside Moustache City, I was graciously allowed to enrol for studies with UNISA. If memory plays me no tricks the subjects were, *inter alia*, the History of Art, Afrikaans, Philosophy and Zulu. One was permitted to procure a number of textbooks and of course I promptly abused this privilege. Thus I got hold of Gombrich's *Art and Illusion*; for me it still is a seminal work when you want to know more about the magic of making paintings, when you recognize the ancient human need for 'writing the self and re-writing the world', or – as Walter Battiss, the late painter associated with this institution, in whose honour I am now speaking, put it – when you start looking for the mechanisms which will enable you to prove that the metaphysical is sometimes more real than the physical. 'For [according to Battiss] this is what art is all about: to shift rivers and to displace mountains . . . Life is sculpted time. By living we fashion time.' (But a French idiom has it that 'Art is work effaced by work.')

My learning of Zulu was promptly stopped. It was explained to me that jailbirds were not to be exposed to 'foreign' languages. (The truth was that they had no reliable warder who could monitor the subject.) Thereafter it was ostensibly feared that we lags would

---

* Ka'afir is an African poet; Hampaté-Bâ was an author and transcriber of oral literature from Mali, who died in 1993.

through our correspondence courses draw succour and comfort from a live world out there — sacrilegious thought! — and the Boere (warders) suspended our leave to be educated altogether.

Which is a pity. Had I been allowed to persevere I might have been better suited to talk about a big subject like Cultural Perceptions and Perspectives in No Man's Land, as I still think of this much vaunted New South Africa. I can only try my best, keeping in mind the country of the heart.

When the dog searches for its bone over such territory it should be with a feeling for place, sense of time, and a suspicious eye on being. What is old and what new in this province where tides have mumbled cavities of time? In his book, *A Minor Apocalypse*, the Polish author Tadeusz Konwicki writes: 'The state owns time; only the Minister of Security knows the real date . . . We were in advance or behind on our production schedules . . . We had this mania to catch up with the West . . .'

The sense of creation is precisely to satiate time and thus to undo it or to lay it away, because no one but ourselves should own our time. We weave into our work the mix of memory — some of it so ancient it may as well belong to the land — and creative intuition. All meaning is making, a blending, a bastardization, a metamorphosis. It is taking hold of time: the only way we know how to gently ease ourselves into the proper position for dying.

But continuing to move and making a noise, more so now that we are trapped in the straits and the defiles of anxiety, remain a prerequisite to survival. Togetherness (as opposed to Apartheid, and you dare not yet speak of unity) is a *movement* harnessing diversity. And national togetherness, in order not to rot into totalitarianism, must be rooted and nourished by cultural variety. Without differences there can be no motion.

In this country without a name — for so long described only as a vague geographical concept, *South Africa*, with its self-digesting history — any progress toward the apparently unattainable utopia will depend on growth toward the embodiment of a South Africanness, more justice and greater freedom, a deeper acceptance of differences and a more spacious recognition of the binding characteristics. These must remain the only way to limit violence and murder. Besides, pushing back the skylines of our journey may be our last chance to prevent a stifling new hegemony from replacing the musty old one. After all, we cannot doubletrack. Behind the dunes lies the toxic cadaver of Apartheid. And thus we arrive at the two poles of the equation which we must bring into play: being alike, being different.

One would like to assume that some immutable premises make a tolerant coexistence compelling, and that these will, as well, effect a mutation of the power relationship through a blending of cultures. *Hic rosa, hic salta* – 'here is the rose, here the dance will be,' Marx (after Hegel) claimed.* The dynamics for the resolution of South Africa's problems lie exclusively within the boundaries and the conscience of the country. To do away with doubt by killing the Other is ultimately suicidal – or am I spouting pious nonsense? Communities are dependent upon one another and they cannot be sundered – or will too much blood drown the connections? The accumulation of past sacrifices, the repeated confirmations of an attachment to different and fairer dispensations, and our shared responsibility toward the dreams of the dead – surely these must guarantee the working out of a more humane future. Or are we underestimating the indifference and the brutalization that will follow upon the coming to power of a single party?

When all is said and done and despite the mutually transformative influences with the coming about of new identities, despite the change of regime – a change with power now residing with cabals and caucuses appealing to a majority hegemony – at sundown and for as long as the inner eye of memory can look ahead, we will still encounter the existence of discernably separate cultural *groups* (identified by languages, customs, perhaps skin colour, or by their stubbornly singular hierarchy of values).

How will the differences be fitted into a larger pattern? Perhaps it will behove us to remember that old sociological dichotomy between community and society, where community relations are seen as natural or primordial because they arise from all manner of shared emotions and traditions that create a fairly homogeneous culture, and where society can be considered a historical construct, defined (according to Max Weber) by a 'rational free market' or 'voluntary associations', in other words by economic necessity or political convenience. Is it too static to reason like this? Now take the black community in America for instance – are its members, after

---

* Another version, brought to my attention, goes: *Hic Rhoda* . . . evidently referring to the Greek island where some hero was dared to jump from a cliff.

a civil war, after a successful struggle for civil rights, after dying *en masse* in overseas wars and after decades of affirmative action, now more integrated than before? And integrated with whom? For what?

The problem of communities coexisting beyond the demise of Apartheid lies on the plane where fear of the Other (the dusky brother or the luminous shadow) – fear of being ousted and superseded, of losing work (through uplifting programmes whereby the old clientelism of jobs for pals will be replaced by the new version of positions for comrades), of a diminution in income and possessions and status, or a fear of the continuation of unfair relations between master and slave, of reduced and inferior liberties, of repression and strife – where all these apprehensions are *real*.

It is not the Mandelas and the Mbekis and the Meyers who will be touched by these misgivings – they already live hand-in-pocket with the Oppenheimers and the Motlanas.* It is the rough, white and black, unpoliticized *lumpen proletariat* who will have to take each other on. (I say 'unpoliticized' in spite of their gun-toting and slogan-mouthing.) They are the ones who will go out with foaming hearts inspired by vague instincts to massacre if they deem themselves to be with their backs to the execution wall. They are the people who will not gain advantages by the corruption of 'liberation', who will reject the pretty psalms of brotherhood and the purported 'civilization' of the prognosticators, and who could eventually rise up in fundamentalist revolt against the party-state. And they too are the ones, when the day is foul with corpses and the playing field steeped in gore, who would have to settle with one another – long after the well-meaning affluent have found refuge along the lakes of Switzerland.

Why is it so difficult for our supposed 'revolutionary' policy makers to incorporate the federal option in their considerations? Is it because territorial demarcation here still carries the stench of Apartheid? Is an unjust sharing-out of wealth feared? Or is it that we, as freedom fighters, still find ourselves in the moment of realizing the booty of a unitary state whose power it is now our turn to exercise – at the crest of the equalization of integration, feeling the

* Winnie Mandela, Thabo Mbeki (ANC spokesman on foreign affairs, first Vice-President), Roelf Meyer (National Party government minister and chief negotiator, a minister in the new coalition government), Harry Oppenheimer (millionaire owner of multinationals like Anglo-American), Ntatho Motlana (millionaire ANC enterpreneur) – as symbols of the old and new élite establishment.

intoxication of the powerful role to be played by the state as central political and economic authority? The state, our jealous cannibalistic god . . .

All the more strange now when there is a growing awareness elsewhere in Africa that the centralized nation state is by definition undemocratic, that it cannot work because the conception and outlines do not fit historical realities and cultural demarcations, and where it seems possible that people will progressively advance toward federalist solutions.

Basil Davidson in his *The Black Man's Burden* comes to the conclusion that: 'A hopeful future . . . would have to be a federalising one: a future of organic unities of sensible association across wide regions within which national cultures, far from seeking to destroy or maim each other, could evolve their diversities and find in them a mutual blessing.' And the Ugandan political theorist Mahmood Mamdani, in an unpublished critical review of Davidson's work, takes the argument a few steps further. Again I quote: 'The point is neither to celebrate "modern tribalism" nor to recoil from it in alarm. Rather, to recognise its contradictory nature is to appreciate the contradictory possibilities in any liberation of "modern tribalism". While any type of federation would have to recognise the legitimacy of "tribal" interests, the resulting "tribalism" could either be democratically-constituted or turn into a top-down manipulation. The outcome, in turn, would depend on whether or not federalism has been joined to "mass participation" through a reform which goes beyond simply federalising the colonial hold over the peasantry to dismantling it . . . For if we are to arrive at a political agenda that can energise and draw together various social forces in the highly fragmented social reality that is contemporary Africa, we need to devise an agenda that will appeal to both civil society and peasant communities, that will incorporate both the electoral choice that civil society movements seek and the quest for community rights that has been the consistent objective of peasant-based movements.'

Let us not forget that the Zulu people still partly live in rural communities, or that the Afrikaners are still peasants – even though their crops were to a large extent the civil service, the mines, the railways and the police.

Do the guys on the extreme right – the *Volkstaters* (adherents to the ideal of a purified Afrikaner state) – constitute the final spasm of a colonialist era, of the time when territorial conquest and racial

domination were considered 'normal' (and which caused the domina-
tor, the boss, to be a rigidly stupid baboon incapable of adapting to
more equitable dispensations)? Or is their thrashing the violent
emergence of a 'new' reality — demanding that room, even geographical space, be accommodated within pluricultural set-ups for
the exercise of group differences?

For forty years we've been hamstrung by this country's official
dogma of 'we are all different and therefore we should be kept
segregated'. Must we now wander for another forty years in the
desert after a new golden calf, a teaching which is as European-
originated as its predecessor and will be enforced in the same
authoritarian and arbitrary fashion, prescribing in the name of non-
racism and non-discrimination that 'we are all the same and should
thus be the subject people of one state'?

The bloody mess of our transitional phase and the contradictions
and discordances erupting like pus ever more violently day by day
must be symptomatic of deeper rifts. All parties sing piously of
moral high grounds (Golgotha?), they speak of converted insights
and they flash their brand new smiles, they fawn and cajole (or
reprimand and warn), they philosophize about affirmative action and
economic take-off like pie in the sky, they console the rich who will
stay rich and promise the poor that they, too, will inherit the earth,
they swish magic wands (looking suspiciously like AK-47s) and dish
out last-ditch increases in salaries, they cheat and lie in our teeth.
We even see the obscene spectacle of the arrogant *Broederbonders*
(members of the semi-secret Afrikaner League of Brothers), who
dumped the country in the shit to start with, now claiming that
they were the ones to open the Damascus road to a new deal. (Like
the fellow who, with good reason, fled from the lion and now
perches high in a tree to pretend for all to hear that he in fact taught
the lion the trick of jogging with him.)

In reality all of these mediocre role players conspire to guarantee
the power monopoly of the political caste, and they agree about the
lowest common denominator of untrammelled access to the state's
feeding troughs — while outside the slaughter continues.

There's grand talk of expressions of national culture where we
have no such thing as a nation. And yet, it is exactly towards a
cultural awareness that we look for spelling out the essential
perceptions of nation building — the complex questions around
identity both local and national, the need for shared ethics allowing

us to coexist peacefully, promoting tolerance and an understanding of the variety of origins and expressions and relationships without which there can be no nation, let alone a valid democracy.

We need cultural awareness for the creative conversion that would transcend these differences and bring about a social and political space for accommodating all the requirements I have tried to suggest here. In other words, we need culture to restrict the state's arbitrary powers and to rein in the bureaucrats and other public parasites. Let me burn my mouth some more: only a vital civil society with the cultural creative process acting as the breath of social consciousness will enable us to drive back to their holes and the cracks in the floorboards the supposed 'security' services – National and Military Intelligence, Mbokodo (the ANC's goon squad trained by the Stasi), the CCB (Civil Cooperation Bureau, our euphemism for death squads) . . . the rubbish and filth and dogshit bedevilling our lives, threatening now to play an even more dastardly role further down the road.

True, that's a mouthful to ask of culture which, practically by definition, has nothing to do with justice; on the contrary, it is permanently in the process of thinking and imagining itself! Creativity is different from explanation; it can neither take the place of nor account for 'something-else'. What I'm really suggesting is that any movement towards a more liveable and supportable situation in this country ought to be a continuous creative undertaking – we are driven for survival towards mixing and self-definition and Other-understanding (and not even Job is as afflicted by definitions as the bastard is), because we revolve around the axis of private *and* public identity (that concept in ideological garb which covers so many atrocities). Our search must therefore not be just a story of political change and economic upliftment. Culture is also concerned, as a thread of remembering and as acts of reconnaissance and recognition and resistance and digestion and transformation. Our lives are inked in by culture because we are in need of recording and modifying our dreams, as also our nightmares, to redirect rivers and to shift mountains. And Battiss's metaphorical mountains and rivers can only be truly grasped, and perhaps crossed, in one's mother tongue.

Since I am now looking for the bone of movement there are a few stones I need to roll out of the way; put differently, there are some stones against which it is my pleasure to lift a leg. 'Culture', 'the people' are among them. (I hear that one nowadays speaks of 'the people and the peasants' in Angola.) The nebulous thing called Culture — I, too, abuse the concept! — must be a devilish spawn of totalitarianism. That use of Culture, preferably organized by 'structures' as an extension of the dominant state ideology, flourished in Nazi Germany and the Soviet Socialist states. In South Africa, too, we are caught between the plague and cholera — between, on the one hand, Apartheid with its patriarchal and colonial tenets of Christian National Education accompanying repression and the censoring of dissidence or deviation (some of us, too, the supremacists decided, were guilty of decadent and degenerate art); and, on the other hand, a potential Stalinism, with its cultural commissars enforcing 'people's culture' as populist idolatry through the appropriate 'structures' — where we must fall into step with historical determinism in the name of 'national' liberation (conveniently forgetting that 'history' is but a majority interpretation by fabrication, the retroactive attempts made by conquerors to impose some inevitability upon the irrational), where we are taught that 'freedom is conforming to the will of the majority' (*eat shit, a thousand flies can't be wrong!*), and where we shall yet again experience the marginalization of dissidents.

Typical of both the old and the new set-ups is our indigenous philistinism — 'good taste' and even better intentions, sentimentalism, anti-intellectualism and 'commitment', mutual moral balls-squeezing and political correctness.

In opposition to the above I'd like to put in my plea for doubt and questioning, diversity, the maintenance of our 'Ho-Chi-Minh trail' of underground tunnels of memory and resistance, tolerance, mixing, blending, crankiness, existentialism, humanism, anarchism . . . to avoid like the plague the tyranny of 'being on the side of the angels'. To forswear ideological cover. As Battiss expressed it: 'To be born vibrant, of restless minds.' To forgo that laziness which Henry James identified as 'the varying intensity of the same.'

It should be clear, I hope, that I don't plead for élitists pulling their meat in ivory towers, nor even for pristine individualism. Locally we also enjoyed an alternative tradition of subversion, you could say of cultural guerilla action; we, too, black and white, rubbed the dog the wrong way. To put it differently, we deserted Calvinism's chilly congregation halls — thanks to small publishers and all kinds of 'alternative' compositions and performances of art. This is the tradition which ought to be deepened and strengthened. How can those of us who fought against the power corruption of the previous regime now shirk the responsibility and sheer joy of opposing without let-up our dear comrades snared in the putrefaction of power under the new rule?

Perhaps the way out lies in a healthy distinction between creativity and education. The most striking transition from the old to the new South Africa is that all those people who until recently had to remain in the background, the majority who existed barely perceptible on the periphery of light, fit only to be removable undesirables or jail fodder, can now step out of the shadows onto the national stage. They are replacing the masters, becoming actors, ringing the changes in equations of power. Their aspirations will now get priority attention. Nobody can dispute the necessity for a redistribution of resources and privileges. They are the ones who must now gain admittance to the opportunities and the possibilities of culture.

But all of that is a matter of education and facilities. The theme song to keep in mind is quite simply social justice: how to, with the accelerating tempo of change, bring about the fine and dynamic equilibrium between programmes of upliftment and old-fashioned competence – and avoid the scornful quota system of 'affirmative action'. It is to be trusted that a pedagogical approach will not lead to the masochistic confusion of art and sociology and ethnography, nor to the hypocritical levelling of arts and crafts advocated by faint hearts and breastbeaters.

Inescapably, social justice is the first law of the land. But the consciousness of a cultural identity is a shared experience as well, a group feeling. There's nothing reprehensible about being simultaneously Afrikaner and South African and African, for instance. The sharpened awareness and required adaptability are indeed among the remarkable challenges of our environment. Surely the creative tension between the conjugating and the centrifugal, between centralism and regionalism, between a binding nationality and variform languages and customs, must be beneficial to unity.

But also, the creative act is, finally, an individual and universal experience, and for that we need free spaces – other permutations of dynamic harmony, of criticism and apostasy and anarchy. The disciplines, the problems and to a certain degree even the themes and motives of creativity — of interpretation and of shaping, of self-knowledge and self-destruction, of othering the self and making of the other — have everywhere and always been the same. And always and everywhere these activities were considered socially and economically to be a luxury, even a burden upon society. Yet, ever since man started looking at himself creativeness became the buried breathing of the community, the option we have of talking to darkness, a road of rhythmed self-discovery, the whittling of god, the murmured adjuration of sun and of moon, the bone belief that we live from death to death, from nowhere to nothing, but that we body forth this knowing in an exploration of life.

Let us not be bothered by the displaying of old Academy foxes or younger political commissars with swaggering tails: when the pot boils it is only normal that froth shall rise. But we shall have to stand fast against the organizers' 'wish for madness', as Lionel Abrahams admonishes us in a recent issue of *Leadership* magazine. He says: 'They have called into being several "structures" to look after culture, and produced innumerable plans, proposals and educated prophecies all apparently resting on a presupposition that activities like the making of poetry, fiction, plays, sculptures, paintings and music are governed by the outcome of theoretical debates and communal decisions, instead of being essentially matters of choice and discovery by individual artists.'

For this country must still be identified. The qualities and the quirks of this country must still be enumerated. Especially under the sombre wing of our century, now when a lowering heaven makes the trees heavier. When fog dissipates we must yet go down to the sea. We have to listen to the mountain's concealed stories and deciper the footprints of those who went before, who vanished leaving only traces of their secret codes encapsulating the euphoria and the terror of exorcism, of feeling the horn of night, they who chose not to be petrified by the power which destroys in order to preserve the shame of ruling. Because we still have to undo power, not through some counterforce, but in the conscious and unconscious flow of tolerance and harmony. Beast, human, god — with failings and with fears, but knowing, too, that we have dreamed ourselves, as free agents of transformation, we have to learn again and again how light espouses the hollows of darkness, how the blade of silence enters the heart to become words. And the *big laugh*, as Nietzsche suggested, as a lyrical vision of the real, is perhaps the only line given to us to establish equity between the void, the great beyond, and our here-and-now.

Pretoria, February 1994

Upon Being Invited to a Conference on Justice and Reconciliation

---

Can Ocells
24 February 1994

To: *Dr Alex Boraine**

Dear Alex,
Just these few words by way of expressing my regret for not being
with you for your important conference. I feel the need to withdraw
into my shell for a while and there to lick my own words as it were.
South Africa is like Commando brandy — even with moderate
consumption the hangover eventually overshadows the euphoria. In
a few days the lady and I are about to retreat from here to Berlin, a
city of dead angels, where I hope to sift through the accumulated
dust of my thoughts.

The fascinating theme you intend to circumscribe may well go to
the heart of our shared human condition: the obligation to live
together in full knowledge of the past with at least a semblance of
decency and tolerance and order, when the foulness of the crimes
committed by some of us against the others is still propagating its
stench. And the questions you will track are lamentably only too
immediate still for too many of us in the Nether world. What
should or could even be done about the horrors perpetrated by man
against man, about the secretion of evil which stained whole
communities — justified, we were told, by considerations of national
security or reasons of state? How did it happen, when we had the
means of flashing back history on our screens of illusion or perusing
it at leisure in libraries with the soft smell of time, that our century
turned out to be so much more totalitarian than any comparable
period of mankind's itinerary? And when a rotten system with its

---

* Until recently director of IDASA, the Institute for a Democratic Alternative in
South Africa; now directing research on the process of reconciliation.

polluted ideology is brought down, or when it flounders in its lues of corruption and cruelty, how is a repetition of the same abuses to be prevented? Can arbitrary force only be checked by counter-force? Can the vicious circle within which we live like snarling dogs be breached? Do we have the capacity to learn from our own vagaries or the mistakes of others? Is full memory a mantra of public protection? Or just the mouthing of self-indulgence? May it not be argued that the more fulsome the memory, the less scope we have for pain and inventive recollection? Isn't our collective lunacy a method for keeping in touch with ourselves? How can the waft of society's moral constraints curtail the power lust of our rulers? And how will total recall and the denunciation of festering injustices shape the syntax of reconciliation? Will a national healing be promoted by lancing the boils? To quote Bertolt Brecht: How can we reconstruct a new house without clearing out the cellars of the old ruin?

I am sure you will hear as many opinions, coloured in many instances by the rancid aftertaste of deprivation and torture, as you have participants. I'd have loved to fit my voice to those of your guests, to compare scars, to test our reciprocal deafness. The struggle goes on, the looting continues, as also the soul-searching and the quest for effective strategies of resistance to barbarism. In our struggle for rehabilitation it is imperative not to trade in tomorrow for today, nor to excuse today's bloodshed in the light of yesterday's darkness. A beginning, I'd imagine, would be to keep active our sense of topography and our understanding of the human desire to belong somewhere.

Had I been present, I should most likely be thinking aloud along the tentative and confused outlines and inlines and lining of my own insights. For example, what juice could be squeezed from the experience of a prolonged sojourn in prison? Apart from an enhanced taste for the grain of contrasts, probably nothing to write home about, and let me assure you that one need not have eaten time in prison to have one's emotions and reactions scrambled! Humiliation, degradation, and ultimately death, can be encountered easily enough. They are old fellow travellers faithfully cooling their heels in taverns along many a road. Similarly, the grace of a deeper breath can as fortuitously be learned under other circumstances. You could have your tonsils removed, or go wait for the dog of God in the rounded silence of some monastery! I'm not even sure about the advantages of being exposed to a knowledge of the misery and the desolation of the human heart – or whether it serves any purpose to hear, ear against the earth, the rattle of bones down the centuries.

To my mind our humanity is defined by being lost and incomplete. The gnawing sense of being unfinished must be due to the fact that our consciousness (as also our expectations) extends beyond death. We just cannot leave eternity alone; why, we even dawdle and diddle with infinitude! The fiddling! We are lost because we reckon ourselves to be civilized members of societies which – shall I say by their very nature? – are revealed to be in discrepancy with the moral precepts we have all been taught to adhere to. Maybe the anguish of repression is caused precisely by those among us who refuse to accept that we're lost, by our guides who are blindly in love with illusions.

In prison I found that man, like other animals, is a product and a spinner of habits. We live by smells, by the return to known places and patterns of reassurance, if not of knowing, and we need to repeat the doodles. Our habits are obsessive, like mating and picking the nose and clinging to superstitions (and our morality is also whistling in the dark while crossing the fingers); even our madness is but the need for *situating* and recognizing where we belong gone haywire (and being recognized, and our supplication for consolation), where obsessional habit-repetition can no longer hold the essential desolation flowing from our awareness of being. Madness is to be drained of all joy.

There is security in patterns, in repeating the known. Much killing is done out of a need for that security. The killing, as in Bosnia and Angola, creates its own looping of the familiar. I kill therefore I am.

We share a scab-picking curiosity, a proxy titillation when piercing the experiences of others, perhaps in the longed-for paroxysmal experience of the Other. The ex-prisoner gets nauseous and tired of explaining what cannot be conveyed (boredom is a cure for a trauma!); he no longer knows what his memory is really like, except sometimes in a dream; he gives what is expected of him, shaded by areas of assumed reference and coded comprehension; he reinvents himself retrospectively because shaping through telling is a transformation, a creation, a making other; he may become an enigma to himself, a secret endlessly slithering out of grasp, but sticking in his own gullet because dunked in the pain and the inadequacy of his own telling; and he obsessively revisits in his own underground the agonizing sequences of failure — 'Where did I make the wrong decisions? How and why did I blind myself? What is the relationship between the intelligent hero I imagined and the cowardly fool peering at me from the mirror?' Words, words like veils. Words — teased and then cut from emotions — constitute the clothing of thoughts. Well, even synthetic cloth will go the way of all flesh to be eaten by moths, and a change in seasons will bring new fashions.

For the onlooker there is the urge to *understand*, thus the better to exorcize and keep bad luck at arm's length, but as well the need (which we label 'cruel') to *see* discomfort in action, to experience what is imagined as a heightened sense of being.

Experiencing being has no moral connotation and teaches no lessons. Besides, survival knows no justice. Even though a simulacrum of justice is often considered the vehicle of survival. The classical example must be how all the suffering of the Jews could not restrain the Israeli state from persecuting and killing the Palestinians. All the blood spilt during the Spanish Civil War did not stop a victorious Franco from continuing to blacken the soil with execution blood. Where leftist regimes came to power propelled by the strength of their humanist convictions, often only monkey respect was shown for elementary human rights.

Man, the two-legged and two-faced conqueror, can apparently be neither changed nor bettered. 'Crimes' (as we stigmatize certain expressions of social behaviour, unless indulged in by the powerful) can only be contained by patterning society in habits of inhibition.

Our *understanding* of events, conceivably also of ourselves, is a process of bringing the disparate into a single frame of reference. It is like taking a photo: the unassimilable, the strange, the foreign and the menacing all become domesticable because artificially focused in a frame of fixed and isolated 'seeing'. The technique of snapping images stops wayward possibilities, causes relationships, suggests sense ... And prevents knowledge, or even only seeing, from leaking all over us!

This, too, you may learn in prison: we all feel the need for ritual and thus for acting. Religion, after all, was originally a matter of theatre. A good voice even today counts for more than true faith. Or will the proximity of the One (the original Other) be measured exactly by the quality of the supplicant voice calling forth? Isn't that why we activists have such sonorous timbre, why our vowels will swell to orotund whining? Is that why we sometimes have South African priests shaking and stomping and prancing with the onanist fury of self-transport?

There is first of all the attempt to placate or to intoxicate, not to *know*. (What we really want to know is the dance of death; to be partner, not prey.) The tragedy in the works of Kafka springs from the tension between the ritualistic – which purports neither to know nor to mean – and the thrust for significance. Maybe ultimate sense lies ensnared in a movement of patterns which lulls understanding to mediate being. We must find the breath for mumbling rhythmically in order to pick our way through the killing fields. This is why, I think, Genet's plays (compare *Le Balcon*) are so essential as articulations of ritual.

One may consider ritual as replacing understanding because it allays the pain of being confronted by the naked image, or as a continuous form of apprehension because it allows illusion to enter the dance with the real. Is understanding not a son of a whore of power? And power the bitch in heat of possession? And possession the mother of truth? And truth the mother of all wars? Is this not finally the purpose and the use of political trials? Is this not why we love birds and must kill them? But ritual is also a shape of power. In fact, power is the ritualistic mating with the void.

I'm deliberately steering away from larger, more formal extrapolations. We are in a mess, erring in the dark whilst conditioned to believe there must be light, yet obliged to go on licking ourselves and our social environment into shape – and inventing a purpose to our efforts. For instance, in South Africa now, people are living on the edge where darkness cuts the light. Indeed, many edges: oblivion, freedom, justice, change ... And trapped in the quicksand of forward movement.

I sometimes think the pattern of rituals also discloses our deep urge for humiliation, for abasement, for the chance of suspending the rules by sliding beyond the limits. The same force is at work in any act of creation. Not to be confused though with the enforced dehumanization of prison life where you will be exposed to instances of degradation and sequences of power abuse *to which you cannot react*, thereby inducing a self-loathing in the witness made impotent.

Poor human cattle that we are! A word of caution nevertheless: Let's not equate the ritual of exposure and confession only with power or with self-pity; we'll be in even darker valleys of death unless we steer clear of victimology, meaning indulging the humble pride and the vanity of the victim, the soul-corruption of suffering. It is vital to keep intact the capacity for rage!

The minimal guideline growing from the minimalist convictions of the sceptic: *It is wrong to kill!* Because the rub-out doesn't solve the riddle of being born alone to die alone. By extension, that it is self-defeating to smother freedom or dreams of decency. Let the riddles multiply! The way forward can never be to commit crimes against the stories of history and culture, nor to stand by when these misdeeds are done.

A Russian proverb apparently states: remarking upon injustice is like having an eye gouged out, looking away is losing both eyes. Heiner Müller, the German playwright, points out that the level of culture is fixed by the way in which society interacts with its dead. We must continue talking to the deceased if only to explain to them why their dreams were groundless and how their sacrifices turned to dust.

The way forward is to keep moving!

With fraternal greetings.

A Reading of Place

Writing is a transcription of the real: in other words, a spinning out of the known or of that which has been experienced. It could reflect shared perceptions; it is often a very private rendering only obliquely hinting at some intimate accretion. Writing also explores the unknown nooks and crannies of our mental surroundings and in so doing it modifies our expectations. By identification it invents the real.

Perhaps I'm particularly aware of this dual capacity of the act of writing — giving account while inventing itself — because it started in all seriousness for me with a moment of embarkation which was also a break with my past.

In the beginning there was leave-taking. I can just about name the date when I found myself suddenly stripped of all previous certainties. Maybe the deflagration of self just came late. At the age of twenty I left behind me a country, a continent, a youth, a language, an identity and perhaps also a memory. What came after would have to be imagined. In due time I realized that the past, too, would need to be invented so as to give depth and coherence to the ongoing. Many years down the road I was to learn that 'identity' was a temporary awareness meeting and mating moment to moment, a line of recognition flowing from the pen and the brush. It would be a shifting alliance of emotions and remembered movements and convictions, an observation point and a conduit of experience, the place where appearance and substance could create a tension of consciousness but which could live only in movement. 'The placing of I', if it may be so described, would in fact be a process. Language was to be the history of sedimentation: a topography of absence. Identity was to be discovered by location. Henceforth the place will be the writing, continually coming into being and dissolution.

Maybe the ear and the eye and the nose and the hand are neutral tools of perception and expression. But the very idea of hearing, or of seeing, and the act of transmission (transgressing the silences of the heart), are conditioned by memories linked to the first awareness of place. This place is not less true and safe for being partially imagined. From the moment when South Africa slipped beyond the horizon and became unattainable it was changed into the bedrock of my experiences.

In a note on autobiotrophy (called *Self-portrait/Deathwatch*) included as an appendix to *Judas Eye*, a volume of poems published in 1988, I tried to describe how my severance from South Africa – and more precisely from a region at its south-western extremity known as the 'Boland', the Upper Country, a land of vineyards and mountains – was a jump into a free fall away from the strictures of my tribe. I then wrote that my expectations, my apprehensions, my instinctive recognition of *the right position and place* (read for this the unquestioned sense of belonging), the means by which I experienced space and rhythm and structure or the way of my relationship to the environment and to other people, my notion of breath and/or breathing space which flows from mountains and a cloud very high in the sea-coloured sky, that which reverberates as 'blue' in me if you were to utter the sign – that this substratum which constitutes the cognitive mechanism of my being was formed during the pre-rational years in Africa.

My very language, Afrikaans – a creole invention spoken and tasted only in those provinces – curled up in memory spaces of resonance as a night-tongue of tenderness and of curses. Being cut off from my youth brought about a land-sickness, a hankering after booming breakers and the mordant wit of a drunken proletariat and ripe stars and the perfume of gardenias embalmirɜ the night on a darkened veranda. South Africa was an obsession nibbling like a subversive dream at the edges of my wakefulness.

It was a paradoxical space though, a zone of pain and conflict. When I returned there I felt exposed and hunted. Who did it belong to? Whose interpretation of its struggles was to carry the day? I'd referred to it as the *paradise* from which I'd been barred – but the disputed garden was rotten with worms. It was *No Man's Land*.

Paris, the station of exile, only surfaced as a flickering mood in my earlier writing. Characters may walk off its busy pavements smeared with dog faeces into my stories, the wind-blown light over its rooftops may be reflected in the pages and you may hear the hum of its smothered, poison-belching arteries behind the words, but I knew I'd forever be a foreigner in this hub of State. Not a stranger: this megapole of intellectual and cultural manifestations so conducive (and irritating) to creative stimulus, is the only town I know really well.

From 1975 to 1982 the locus of my writing became as circumscribed as a bottomless well. Arrested during a clandestine visit to Paradise and sentenced for 'terrorism', I entered South Africa's prison world as if traversing a mirror. This then was the true heart of the country, the belly of the beast, a parallel universe complete with its own colours, smells, sights and sighs, myths, stories, dreams, relationships. The language was both hackneyed and in constant metamorphosis. Death House, the Abattoir — all these walled cities of incarceration became blurred and concentrated in my mind as *The Place. The Place* also grew on the page. Not as if there were any such thing as exorcism. Prison is the crucible of unmaking. *The Place* taught me the cold and splendid lesson that survival comes at the price of feeding small morsels of oneself to death.

I don't know whether the subconscious place took shape then or earlier. For many years I remember having recurring dreams of finally reaching 'home'. Often the route would climb through narrow defiles sucked clean like a black tooth by some wind of eternity, and I'd arrive for the first time in the familiar place — a partly destroyed or half-built town with the world falling away at its feet. My throat would tighten with elation and a savage sadness. Sometimes a shadowy companion guides me there, and he or she is either blind or maimed.

And now, for nine years, a free place where the mind moves most naturally is forming a new kernel to my work. Lady One and I go to watch the seasons from an old house (whose stones are petrified roses) on a hill in Catalonia. There I relish the sense of catching the wind, of growing old in another country, of facing a Chinese landscape shifting into focus and then forgetting itself like a dream folding into memory, a thought washed away in shades of pale ink. Like Rimbaud I boasted for a long time of possessing every possible landscape. There I know that I own nothing, that the mind can be a mirror to nothingness, that the landscape itself is a heart of coming and going to be bequeathed to a beloved.

Paris, 12 October 1994

To the Invisible Guests

I have been given the intimidating task of opening the Twenty-Fifth Poetry International Festival, to mumble a few words of welcome and appreciation on the threshold as I invite you in.

It is an impossible commission. Nobody can interpret twenty-five years just as no one can give a single comprehensive definition of poetry or explain why (or even how) people will forever continue stringing words together in order to give shape and colour to silence. Besides, when one opens a door you should do so quietly and quickly and then stand aside.

As the door swings open – what is it that we bring here? What do we take away? Perhaps we only carry empty frames for the photos we shall take of the landscapes as seen from the rooms where we loved, and not of the faces of the loved ones.

I shall not name any names, neither to commemorate the dead nor to thank the living, hosts and guests, who meet in this place. Because we are all one body, one bird, and therefore all one absence. Or will it be unfair to leave unspoken even the softest whisper of muddy footprints on white paper?

When a door swings open we hear wind, a rush of nothingness; but also – as in rain coming down from distant mountains, in the voices and faces of all those we loved, the forefathers and the descendants – the naked memories of friends come back to the naked brown earth. This is how absence becomes a bird. This is the way a river flows from the ocean to the mountains. If you listen carefully you will hear, even in the movements of my hand, quotes and snippets of sighs and cries from the ancestors as from contemporaries.

This room is too small to accommodate all the shades gathered here with us: ancient Chinese sages with wind in their empty robes and wine mixed with poetry on their breaths; drifters over snowy plains with frost tinkling in their beards; those living in prisons and camps and forests and exile who listen to the thud of axes on wood; women through the ages shaping the heart's freedom; Dutch poets and publishers who had the grace of never taking themselves seriously; those who knew the intimate lining of night and others who could look into the sun until their eyes were black holes digesting experience; those who wrote flowers with amateur bodies; they who lived in an imaginary Europe which is now of stone, of sea and of a sensation of overwhelming exhaustion; those who spat flames and then tasted the ash of their tongues; those who made love with death so as to give birth to words; the young ones who dreamed of visiting a country so young it hadn't yet decided on its name and its flag; and those who die as figs die in autumn, shrivelled and full of themselves and sweet. We greet them all.

We are indeed celebrating the future of the past. Nobody knew, back in 1970, what Poetry International would look like today. The product, the process, was a group effort, fragile but resilient, in itself a homage to the perenniality of poetry. Somehow the strength of weakness was found the way grass will adopt the breathing of seasons. It is said that the tongue has no teeth, but it bites deeper. May it always be so.

Every poem is the memory of all poetry. Similarly, a site of creation (of transmission and transgression) is also always one of remembering. Our poem is twenty-five years old. Somewhere we should have a public list, a scroll, a wall, a totem pole, rekindling all the voices associated with this poem. Gradually then the city will be dotted with names stroked by seawinds and bleached by the reflection of light from water and window and mirror, each name evoking a personal line of feeling the way into the dark.

Why is our room so important to us? Because it is an oasis to which we may return again and again to find water (and the sounds of water) after a dusty year's travelling through the deserts of office and academia and isolated workroom. Because it is a place where we praise the virtues of disobedience and practise the gentle art of a permanent revolution which can only threaten the powerful and the cruel, a cool spot under the trees where we may share the sacred privilege of laughing at death. Because it is that too: a paradise of sorts. We know species die, and sometimes a whole people will disappear. When poets die they go to Rotterdam. Death and resurrection are yearly events. This is why our dead friends are alive.

Let our festival then also be the occasion of writing the names of this tribe of wanderers who lay claim to no territory, who will never go to war for any gain or cause.

All we ask of our hosts is that they should keep the frontiers and the doors open. Don't retreat behind your walls. Don't make lost dogs of the refugees coming through. And don't expect them to conform to the self-disgusting role of professional victims or exiles. We are not sufferers. The world is a sorry place — but there can be no reason why we should ever feel sorry for ourselves. As poets we ask no privileges. We only accompany the people, we only try to demolish time by singing on the road. After all, the word is the first step of freedom from oneself.

I want to cite someone whose words brought the menace of death, who is now hiding for his life. 'Writers [he wrote recently] are citizens of many countries: the finite and frontiered country of observable reality and everyday life, the boundless kingdom of the imagination, the half-lost land of memory, the federations of the heart which are both hot and cold, the united states of the mind (calm and turbulent, broad and narrow, ordered and deranged), the celestial and infernal nations of desire, and, perhaps the most important of all our habitations — the unfettered republic of the tongue ... These countries we can claim, truthfully and with both humility and pride, to represent.'

Of course we have responsbilities. As our century draws to a close we cannot allow it to be said that it was but a stain on the book of times — a welter of barbarism, invasions, exploitation, ethnic purification, extermination camps, the death of forests, historical amnesia. We can show that there was also laughter and love, that some tried to pen down the bird's cry and keep alive a memory of decency and tolerance, and thus that poetry too was stitched like a line of light on the robe darkened by blood ... even though we knew how much easier it was to lay down a line of darkness. And that we shall let go reluctantly, as when some line on a page is loved and it is hard to turn and continue reading the never-ending story. The story which is so beautiful it has a long way still to go.

Poetry at least serves the purpose of showing us how difficult it is to remain one and the same person. Because our house is open, in the door there's no key, and it is a coming and going of invisible guests.

What I have said here is neither my own nor is it poetry, that I must admit. For poetry is only written from time to time with much resistance, under unbearable pressure and in the hope that we do not serve as tools to the bad, but only to good spirits.

Rotterdam, 20 June 1994

The Memory of Birds in Times
of Revolution

In the morning I get up with the intention of putting in a good day's work. It is still early, but already the outside is made limitless by light. Birds are singing in the trees of the neighbourhood. One must not waste the presence of light, it is a precious commodity, I remind myself. This I always tend to forget because there is so much of it right now, hiding in the trees, blinding the windows, pouring through the streets. One must hide in the light in order to be able to see, in fact to be the surface. The texture, I should say. Say the text face. I am the surface of what I see, I say to myself. And I hear the birds answering a pattern of dappled descriptions. It is the nature of birds to be answering machines. When you telephone a thought to an absent friend, or a dead one, or one who is making love — the bird tells you to speak after the beep. Why is there so much light? It must be because we are living on the edge of the world, being set ablaze by the sun. When we dream, there are sparks streaking the vaults of infinity. Or maybe there is a revolution somewhere just beyond the definition of perception, so ardently desired and of such transformational importance that it lights up the skyline. Perhaps it is but the memory of an event which brightened the expectations of people, a memory of the future, the way Mozart's music takes you through the hooded no man's land of death into the light of bird-sounds beyond. All flying is a memory of flight. Did night ever fall? I seem dimly to remember a dream of flames like wings: birds must have been sending out coded messages into the void, in which case it couldn't have been dark. When I wake up my hands are black.

This is enough. I have the intention of putting in a good day's work after all. Already I am in the room where the elements of creation are kept — the paper, canvas, glue, colours, pencils, brushes, ideas, echoes and memories. Light floods the working space with the diffusion of seeing. It will be up to me to marry that light to a surface of signs or metaphors. You must take off light's bridal gown if you want to feel the texture of her skin and to let your bird explore her tree of paradise alive with shadows and mirrors. Where to start? Images rise to the surface – of broken tongues and of whales wearing bow-ties and of politicians sounding the hollow drum of their convictions and of bankers ascending alive to heaven in shiny limousines and of horses gently kissing cherry blossoms and of a friend sleeping with death and of people blackened by fire before they are hanged from scaffolds to scare off the birds, like commas being killed by silence. This is of no use to me, I say, and I hear the birds go yes-yes and no-no. This is not what painting is all about. I cannot paint Africa or that crackling of the mind which singes the wings. I can only paint a painting. Although it is true that every thought must come to mind sooner or later, sometimes because of utter exhaustion, it is not equally true that everything can be thought. A revolution cannot be thought. And when it is imagined it will only be as the memory of birds. Birds don't have to invent flying.

By now I realize that I am skirting the painful process of decision-making which is creation. I must get around to drawing a hand, an eye, a look, the violence of a wingbeat, perhaps an absence. So now I shall sharpen the pencils and line them up, rinse the brushes and change the water, half-close the eyes to size up the limitless space of the square sheet caressed by light. My thoughts flit from object to object. What is this revolution the birds keep singing about? When I haven't said anything? Will it ever come? This could be a beginning. Maybe somebody will call me.

I bend my gaze, my hand swoops down to scratch the paper or the canvas the way a bird does when it is looking for a worm. There are many worms and dead friends just below the surface. One should never give up hope. Time has passed again and again. It is good to sharpen the pencils. Tomorrow – of this I am sure – I shall put in a good day's work. Now I shall dream. I smooth my feathers, wrap drawings around my hands, and go to bed with a memory of light.

Berlin, May 1989

Acknowledgments

A section of 'Writing the Darkening Mirror' was previously published in Berlin's *Wochenpost*; parts of the text have been with me for some time.

'Tortoise Steps' was a paper presented at an International PEN meeting in Lugano, Switzerland, in May 1987.

'Nelson Mandela Is Free!' was printed in various European newspapers, and under the title 'The Joy of Freedom' in *Altered State*, A Guardian Book, London 1990.

'Fragments from a Growing Awareness of Unfinished Truths' was presented (in Afrikaans) at Stellenbosch University, South Africa, on 16 August 1990; it was later published in a small manual called *Hart-lam* (which could be translated as either 'Sweetheart' or 'Dead heart').

'The Long March' was a paper presented for the conference *Home: A Place in the World*, at the New School for Social Research, New York, 25 October 1990, and subsequently printed in other journals.

'Cadavre Exquis' was written for the catalogue of an exhibition, *Self-portraits and Other Ancestors*, at Stockholm's Kulturhuset, 1991.

'Painting and Writing for Africa' was read at the Kulturhuset, Stockholm, on 27 January 1991.

'An Open Letter to Nelson Mandela, 16 April 1991' was published in the South African *Sunday Times*.

'An Open Letter to Nelson Mandela, 17 May 1994' was published in South Africa, Holland, France and Germany.

'Thinking Fire' was a contribution to the conference 'Nature and Culture', organized by the Netherlands Unesco Commission, June 1992; it was later published in the New York magazine *Grand Street*.

'Cold Turkey' was published in the *New York Times Book Review*.

'The Shattered Dream' was published in 'The African Past and Contemporary Culture', No. 8 in the series *African Literatures in English*.

'Dog's Bone' was given as a memorial speech at the University of South Africa on 14 February 1994, in honour of the painter Walter Battiss; it was later published in the *New York Review of Books*.

'A Reading of Place' was published in *The Washington Post Book World*.

'The Memory of Birds in Times of Revolution' was a text written for an exhibition and printed in a limited-edition catalogue in Berlin, May 1989.